Spirits of the Age:
Poets of Conscience

SPIRITS OF THE AGE
POETS OF CONSCIENCE

EDITED BY MONA ADILMAN

QUARRY PRESS

Proceeds from the royalties on sales of this book will be donated to the *Index on Censorship* and *P.E.N. International.*
The publisher thanks The Canada Council and the Ontario Arts Council for financial assistance in producing this book. Special thanks to the *Index on Censorship* for cooperation in securing permissions to publish many of the selections in this book and in verifying biographical information on the poets.

Canadian Cataloguing in Publication Data

Main entry under title:

Spirits of the age

(International poets series)
Includes bibliographical references.
ISBN 0-919627-07-2

1. Poetry, Modern — 20th century. 2. Political prisoners — Poetry.
3. Political poetry — 20th century.
I. Adilman, Mona Elaine, 1924-   . II. Series.

PN6101.S73 1989   808.81'9358   C89-090299-2

Edited for the press by Linda Bussière.
The cover features the woodblock "On the way to the Trenches" by Nevinson [1915]. Design and imaging by ECW Production Services, Sydenham, Ontario, Canada. Printed and bound in Canada by Hignell Printing Limited, Winnipeg, Manitoba.

Distributed in Canada by University of Toronto Press, 5201 Dufferin St., Downsview, Ontario M3H 5T8, and in the United States of America by Bookslinger, 502 North Prior Avenue, St. Paul, Minnesota 55104.

Published by *Quarry Press, Inc.*, P.O. Box 1061, Kingston, Ontario, Canada K7L 4Y5, and P.O. Box 348, Clayton, New York, U.S.A. 13624.

CONTENTS

INTRODUCTION

Spirits of the Age presents in translation the best work of poets from around the world who have been imprisoned, tortured, exiled, or otherwise oppressed because of their writing. These "poets of conscience" are internationally recognized not only as spokespersons against political oppression but also as highly accomplished artists. Their experience of oppression would seem to charge their poetry with a voice that speaks to all mankind, with a vision that transcends political boundaries. Not surprisingly, poets of conscience such as Jaroslav Seifert, Claribel Alegria, and Kim Kwangsŏp have been awarded the Nobel Prize for Literature, the Casa de Las Américas Prize, and the Korean Academy of Arts Prize, respectively.

Oppressive regimes obviously distrust culture, fear poets. In so-called police states poets are a primary target for attack because they are considered a perennial danger to the status quo. The poet sings of justice, freedom, and compassion, thus alienating the government that abuses justice, quashes freedom, perverts compassion. The poet becomes "an enemy of the state." The poems in this anthology have been written by such *enemies* of the state, by prisoners of conscience in countries where writers are often given sulphur injections to keep their lips from moving, where poets are silenced by "medicinal stunning," where poets are transformed into "camp dust."

How shall we match the poet to the crime? Human rights activists are arrested for "hooliganism." Signatories of Charter 77, the petition signed on behalf of prisoners of conscience, are imprisoned for subversion. Love of one's language is a crime against the state. Even songs are blacklisted and tarred with the brush of anti-state slander. Criticism of the secret police is called anti-revolutionary. Manuscripts are confiscated, their writers tortured until they lose control of their bodily functions. Other writers simply "disappear."

But the poetry survives in memory, in *samizdat*, passed from hand to hand like rat-scraps in prison, until it is finally dropped outside the walls and published in "padlock editions."

Prisoners of conscience share a superhuman courage in the face of atrocity — the will to tear away the gag of censorship and write the truth. When Vasyl Stus, the Ukrainian poet, wrote, "I accuse the KGB of depriving my people of their tongue and their voice," his poetic courage matched the scientific courage of Galileo, who was imprisoned for his claim the earth was round when the church and state believed otherwise. When the cry of the poet's soul resonates, we identify with Armando Valladares in the Republic of Cuba, Mang Ke in the People's Republic of China, Ahmed Fouad Negm in the Arab Republic of Egypt. Suffering is a universal language in the Republic of Malawi, or in the Socialist Republic of Vietnam, in the Republic of Guatemala, or in the Union of Soviet Socialist Republics. Writers like Ahmad Faraz in the Islamic Republic of Pakistan, Abdellatif Laābi in the Kingdom of Morocco, and Saeed Soltanpour in the Islamic Republic of Iran are all "spirits of the age." Poets in prison form a powerful link in the chain of humanity, a spiritual bonding with all that is human, with all hope of survival under the heel of oppression. Their poetic vision transcends barbed wire and psychiatric prisons.

The *Index on Censorship*, *P.E.N. International*, *Amnesty International*, the *Helsinki Monitoring Group*, and other bodies struggle to draw attention to the plight of prisoners of conscience, arguing that the persecution of any writer in any country is a disgrace to all nations, an indictment of all mankind. *Spirits of the Age* likewise draws attention to this fact in presenting the extraordinary artistic achievement of poets of conscience. Their spirit has passed through bars, beyond the forces of censorship. Their spirit speaks to us of the eternal passion of the human soul for liberty and beauty on this earth, where freedom of expression must become an inalienable right.

Mona Elaine Adilman
Montreal, 1989

"Literature is fire; it is a form of permanent insurrection and recognizes no straitjackets. The more terrible and cruel an author's writings against his country, the more intense the passion that binds him to it."

Mario Vargas Llosa *Republic of Peru*

VASYL STUS *Union of Soviet Socialist Republics*

What love! A whole eternity has passed
since I did love and dream from day to day,
that all would merge and memory bypass,
parting, to the last comma and contraction learned.
But once again I go into that cell among
the melancholy willow's boughs. I will await
some kind of random and unknown feelings
which will turn virtue into shame.
And there will be parting enough for two,
and there as well will be a silent joy —
to feel with the whole heart the long debt
owed to a past with a white headboard,
where a pair of ebony braids still flow,
and a pair of long arms, drunk upon the dark,
and a pair of lips, with passion greedy,
suddenly send us headlong down the slope
of idiotic virtue. Beneath the sorrow and beneath
the wing of some most saintly sinner,
who gifted us with those kinds of rooms
where sleep is no disgrace and love — no shame,
where everything is there for give and take,
and in the middle of the night one can exceed
the bounds of self.

The twilight gloaming fell
and wove together soul and sleepy earth.
The hoarded chorales of my loneliness
litter before me my entire road.
And wherever I go, wherever I aspire —
the piney twilight freezes overhead.
I keep a lookout for my long-awaited fate,
but I'll not see it — I'll retire from the game.
Now there's a game: Firebrands fly,
Teeth chatter from the force of manic laughter,
Laugh out the other side — things will be better,
(and if worse — that also is no sin).
Why should I curse you, my misfortune?
I do not curse. I cursed not. I'll not curse.
Let life be but one stubbled field,
but I will not neglect to cross it.
I'll make it to the edge. Be it upon my hands,
be it on elbows, crawling — little matter,
I may scuff up my soul against the rocks —
all the same there is naught sweeter
than this lost and indolent,
than this carefree, repellent, than
this earth, which alone gives me meaning
and which brings colors to my tears.

Here, it appeared, the sun had never shone.
Till shortly of a sudden came a spray: lilacs
in full bloom gleamed, bronze-bodied pines
gushed at the crown, sipping in the day,
until the shrieks ran down into the humid
valley, where frogs sat dreaming.

Here time stands still. Here the oak
for an eternity gives proof of its old age,
and the contorted hornbeams writhe,
and mountain-ash, like fish, dive
headlong gently down into the depths,
observing with the swallow's gaze
the timeless world and their own timeless age.

Live here a while, and you will see
Ukraine is still a home for nightingales,
and you may glimpse a wood nymph in the glade,
her arms extended, reaching for a squirrel,
and hear a flute sing out across the foothills:
there, there, Lukash may suddenly appear.

Here is a forest — like eternity. Guard it
against your wantonness, your superstition
against your own wasteful stupidity . . .
Here every stump holds in its palm
a nightingale, airy as a song.

Leave yourself at the gate and go,
open and resonant like an untilled field,
observe and listen, take in the perfumes,
and with your hands, in awe,
touch every blade of grass.

Here like a tub of hops, you will ferment,
you will ferment on song, on bees
that gather the sun's glow into themselves,
that by the day consumed, still live
upon that day, not subject to the age old laws,
as if on gifts, they live upon the loss.

Come here and learn in silence
to live a human life. From the trees
learn goodness, as a gift to self.
To speak when there is need to speak. Be silent
when silence is the rule. And all your life to smile
so that — still smiling —
you can meet with death.

translated by Volodymyr Hruszkewycz

IRINA RATUSHINSKAYA *Union of Soviet Socialist Republics*

3

Our terms have not yet been served
Our spirits have not been proved
And when the birds take flight
We are not ashamed of our songs
Through this lunatic town we wander
In the ugly clothes of the age
And our small sorrows
Twist on little dry paws.
Harmless witnesses!
We're not worth a shot in the back.
Unprompted, we leave in silence
Snuffing the candles behind us.
How we love to guess what will be
What will follow our mute departures!

Perhaps the nights will be different
And no one will notice the wind?
Maybe summer will turn out cold —
And our poets will be forgotten?
And our tears will remain unrealised
And our faces will be dispersed
And our lips will not be remembered
That have known no kisses!

Hapless children of the age
We depart, wishing only this
That someone, from pity,
Should burn our letters, unread.

With what care we extinguish the candles
So that wax should not spot the linen!

translated by Sally Laird

8

Two versts from the Dvina's shore —
A bullet in your throat —
In your final torment —
In the midst of your war —
You stretched out your arms forever

And on your white shirt — your blood is blue
And your mouth bitten through
And the ants, perplexed —
Simple souls —
Dance in a ring.

Not future summer days
Nor bitter posthumous glory
But the grass will bewail you
In the conquered depths
Your thunder has flown.
Our fate is to walk in shame
In their vile processions
But your eyes were bequeathed to me
As a curse
And a recompense.

translated by Sally Laird

20

The Palace Square parade is met by
Such an unflattering rain!
The placards on the walls get runny
With something sticky imbruing the high
face of Lenin.
The raised flags soar
As criminal runnels descend
Over the slogans,
   the posters,
     the paper —
Like the smoke of the deadly diamond
Over an executioner's block.
The faces, already eyeless as silhouettes,
Still do to frighten children with that look.
The Palace parade drags past — sluggish puppets
Crashing in step on the asphalt streets.
The Square is obeisant, sick,
Its eyes squeezed tight, no window
Open to the perimeter of black
Blood and red mob — any minute now
The mob — at a word — could close in, turn
Into animals, desert their places . . .
But no — they dare not — a stubborn
Angel sternly lifts up a cross.

translated by Pamela White Hadas and Ilya Nykin

Stars suddenly rain down, and the heavens are filled with cold
The moon is wavering — hold on, don't loosen your grip!
Close your eyes — out there, beyond your weary vision
A skater inscribes his rings, precise as compasses.
Shades vanish in the black-and-white engraving of winter
Grim, beggared phrases rumble with a verb.
Five steps to the window, four from wall to wall
And an eye winks absurdly, framed in the iron door
Monotonous, sly, the interrogation drags by
The young escort has a soldier's artless crudity . . .
Oh what peace — to wander through winter in silence
Not letting a single 'no' pass sore, cracked lips
The pendulum of snow has failed: what week is this?
But my eyes have dimmed on the page and my head is burning.
Through the heat and the chill I shall stagger my way to April!
I'm on my way. And God's hand is on my shoulder.

translated by Sally Laird

31

And we remain —
In place on dreadful chessboard squares —
All of us prisoners.
Our coffee
Smells like burned letters
And post offices
Smell like opened letters.
City blocks are deaf —
And there's no one there to shout:
'Don't!' And the chiselled faces
On façades have their eyes shut.
And every night
Birds are flying away from the city.
And blindly
Our dawns drench with light.
Wait!
Is it just a dream? Could it be?
But in the morning
Newspapers hit the street.

translated by Pamela White Hadas and Ilya Nykin

32

With what power and tenderness
Time grips us by the shoulders
And freedom tears the mouth to tatters —
The plain, and the spurs —
We're off like a shot —
What a life, what happiness!
What a brilliant fate —
The inspired liar will write
With his non-historical bias.
So even seven-year-old boys
Will weep over our "once-upon-a-time,"
Ready to pay the same price
For hopes that are the same —
Just anyone, from any parts . . .
A house of hobbles, a path of hearts.

translated by Pamela White Hadas and Ilya Nykin

I will write about the despondent
Who stayed behind on the shore.
Of those sentenced to be silent
I will write.
And then I'll make a fire.
O, how these lines will soar up,
The pages fall back to ash
Under the savage slap
Of a long-lapsed emptiness!
With what an arrogant gesture
I will be outstripped by the flame!
And the foam of ashes will quiver
But nothing will be born from them.

translated by Pamela White Hadas and Ilya Nykin

Distance

I am a wall here,
you a flower there.
Between us a hill
of ice has grown.

In a dream of spring gossamers
that hill dissolves.

Spring is distant as I
wait. Wanting flowers
I walked into the florist's shop.

Flowers followed me out, and perch
on my table.
Spring too has followed after.

There is no distance.
Say there is, and spring dissolves it.
Come or go,
distance is the waiting.

I'm so inept when it comes to a pack!
My grandma could manage.
As though our worldly possessions surpass
Rag-sized dimensions.
Who needs a suitcase?
The notebooks are burnt,
Bread has gone moldy.
But still we execute travellers' rites,
Tying bundles with criss-crossing knots
By our own method.
God bless! — all ready.
Weightless, we leave blades
Of grass unblemished.
We won't return, and we won't upbraid.
Why show our sorrow to people at odds
With an ascension?
From the aridity somebody's slave
Chokes in the background.
Why should we hesitate in the last stage?
We fill a canvas as stylized shapes,
Granted no pathos.

translated by Susan Layton

My Lord, what can I say that's not been said?
I stand beneath your wind in a burlap hood.
Between your breath and pitch-dark plague-dark cloud —
Oh Lord, my God!

At my interrogation what will I say
If forced to speak, to face the country's way —
Deaf, mute, in the body's rags, bruised nearly dead —
Oh Lord, my God!

How will you dare to judge?
Which law is true?
What will you say when I come, at last burst through —

Stand, my shoulder propped against the glass wall —
And look at you,
And ask nothing at all.

translated by Pamela White Hadas and Ilya Nykin

Spirits of the Age

The radio emits a barrage of mysterious crackles,
Leaving us in the dark.
". . . prison sentence . . ." But who? How long?
Here we sit at the glossy, fragile table, while an angel
Watches sadly, dishevelled in clouds of the cigarette smoke

But just whom does he think he'll protect —
This exotic, untutored
Bird so clumsily plumed?
Eyes much darker than seen in these parts,
Inconversant with usual sessions of weeping and terror —
An unsummoned arrival — this orphan,
This traveler with wares!

Flying between the door and the chain,
Will he light on a shoulder?

Why should he share suffocation,
And silently learn to displace
Daily doles with the rations of jail,
Shed old clothing for tatters,
Taking regular bars for the filagree work of a fence?

Why get caught in a nightmarish world
Where the snow goes on rampage,
And biography runs from the birthday to riflemens' squad?
Knowing nothing, he sleeps
With his palm as a shield from the lamplight,
Undisturbed by the static.
No need for adjusting the sound.

translated by Susan Layton

Poets of Conscience   *31*

MYKOLA RUDENKO   *Union of Soviet Socialist Republics*

It's so easy: just recant
And restore your right to live.
A dozen words or maybe phrases
And yesterday will suddenly be brought back:
The trees and flowers in shimmering dew,
And children's voices outside the window;
The fish in the lake and birds in the sky,
And the taste of a kiss on your lips
As proof of love and goodness that exists . . .
Only you no longer will be the same.
Hunched and grown pale from illness,
Just an empty shell without a soul.
Try on the old suits once more,
And get the most out of your study-haven.
Tramp up and down the garden path —
But you won't retrieve the soul you've lost.
Just a dozen words forced out while half-awake
And you are no more,
Just emptiness —
A dungeon concealed in a man.

As long as I live — no one will take away
My truth and my freedom.
And even after death that which I have earned
On the holy field will not die.

No one will take away my treasures,
Even though my body may be taken from me.
I grew with my heart, and did not become callous
And before it, even prison bars are weak.

I brought the whole world to this threshold —
The dawns battle with darkness within me.
A slave is one who does not preserve the soul
And becomes its two-legged prison.

If you have seen the sky within yourself
Then sight cannot be taken away from you.
If there will be no eyes —
   the heart will become the one with vision,
Your soul will rise up to the stars.

They can lock up only our body,
But the spirit will fly throughout the ages.
For a heart which has encompassed the whole world,
No one has forged yet a lock.

It will burn through walls, tear away the shackles,
Throw away the raving beasts.
And one day the Lilliputians will see,
How Gulliver walks above them.

I matured and became enlightened.
Captivity for me does not exist
And words don't die on closed lips.
My spirit lives, like the wind in the field,
A winged infant soaring o'er the world.

I see through the sun, I see so far
That I am indifferent to all of my sorrow.
I do not moan in grief, in despair I do not weep
And do not bloody my mouth with grinding teeth.

I threw away fear, became indifferent to pain.
Secret stars twinkle in my bosom.
I once lived in the world. Now, with freedom lost,
I became the whole world . . .
And the world lives in me.

Poetry is no joke.
She
Is also a cosmic battle.
She is both a mother and a wife,
An oath and a prayer . . .

There is body, mind and soul,
And all this yearns for movement.
Poetry leaves for us
Live crystals of spirit.

And every such crystal
Is not a piece of paper:
In it there is the astral fury of fire,
The birth of galaxies.

If in the midst of new machines
There will be no poetry,
Sons will be reduced to cyborgs,
And people
To automatons.

from Enlightenment, *1978, and* Behind Bars, *1980*
translated by Irena Eva Mostovych

IV

Myron's dark locks turned white by morning:
From forty farms —
No one survived . . .
Just distant megaphones kept roaring
About "new roads" and "Party pride."
    And, wild with words, like lashes raining,
    A well-known poet,
    In killing fits,
    Into one ditch cursed all Ukrainians:
    "Stick and kill! Kill and stick!"
Myron plods on, with horror stricken,
His conscience crucified inside.
Far up ahead, he hears dogs barking —
Thus, someone's left . . . perhaps alive!
    A yard appears — a dray, raked flooring,
    A white-washed doorway, ricks of hay, —
    And, through the door, plump girls alluring —
    Tote buttered dumplings stacked on trays!
A table packed with food stands sagging —
Good whiskey, pickles, pork in brine.
A peasant, shod in clogs of twine,
Stands turning straw inside a wagon.
    Hauling out a samovar before him,
    His cap he cocks and starts inside:
    "Hey! Take that kettle back. It's foreign:
    It's Kurskan — not the Ukrainian style!"
Who screamed those words so strange, commanding
This Hellish travesty of sin?

Then Myron gasped with understanding:
Why, it's a movie set — being filmed!
   And all cleared up, each clue he'd noted:
   Some tribe from Kursk was hired en masse,
   And — robed in bright Ukrainian clothing —
   Railed down to film this staged "repast."
As though to say, let kurkul liars
Desist with their distortions bold,
"that half Ukraine is starved and dying" —

There's been no famine here, —
Behold! . . .

   And now the "kingpins" enter, strolling
   Like lords to gorge on wines and spuds.
   The squares are packed. Standing room only.
   And each man's foreign. Alien blood.

from **The Cross,** *1968*
translated by Roman Tatchyn

LOTHAR HERBST *Polish People's Republic*

Letter 7

I am swallowed up by darkness
and yet surrounded
by a dazzling glow
when I look at the faces
worn out by the vigil, waiting for tomorrow,
when I see the sheets of newspapers
filled with hymns of praise
for the ordinary man —
that includes myself —
when breathing is about to cease
because air has been locked away
behind barbed wire
and only an anecdote occasionally
soars, wheels round and on reaching the target
contracts and falls
at the feet of the guardians of my order of things
and of our system
the mirror alone
that guardian of my conscience
still shows some trace of breath
yet how long
will the dialogue last
in the light — bright and searching —
because it is my own

from the series: Letters About Faith and Hope

JAROSLAV SEIFERT *Czechoslovak Socialist Republic*

Prologue

It's no easy thing to be a poet.

He finds a silver-tongued bird
hovering above its woodland nest
but can't help recalling
— oh, the sinful pleasure —
the warm and tousled hollow
in the armpit of his lover.

He goes further into the woods
lured by imagined voices
while everything shivers round about
And incredibly —
   Quite close he sees
the downy laps of young girls,
first one, then another
retreating, till they disappear from view,
leaving only desire behind.
But no,
   they're nothing but leaves and blossom
and the pink-hued trunks of pines
shimmering after the rain.
It is most beautiful in daytime
and then at night.
   But not I!

Once upon a time the poet spoke
and there came a roar of blood.
Men hastened to their weapons
and women unhesitatingly cut off
their honey and copper-colored locks
to make bow-strings.
They are more springy than those made of nylon.
These days, women's hair is too short
as so at least they make balsam
for human wounds
   and hasten to the wounded,
to bring back their bloodied heads
on the stretchers of their breasts.

Should the tyrant fail to fall
   — this, too, is inherited —
the poet is condemned to silence
and iron bars will, like a hand,
gag his mouth with their claws.
Yet will he shout his verses through the bars
while the wreckers of books
go speedily to work.
   But not I!

Sometimes he will pound word against word
in desperation, to strike a certitude,
but there are none in this world.
In vain he casts his burning words
into the distance, well beyond death,
to shake the silent mysteries,
to set fire to the darkness, which remains still
in the mass grave, merely attaching itself
to the wretched bones
stained with the copper of the cigarette-lighter
they forgot to remove
from the shot man's trouser pocket.

But not I!

from The Casting of the Bells, *1967*

And Now Goodbye

To all those million verses in the world
I've added just a few.
They probably were no wiser than a cricket's chirrup.
I know. Forgive me.
I'm coming to the end.
They weren't even the first footmarks
in the lunar dust.
If at times they sparkled after all
it was not their light.
I loved this language.

And that which forces silent lips
to quiver
will make young lovers kiss
as they stroll through red-gilded fields
under a sunset
slower than in the tropics.

Poetry is with us from the start.
Like loving,
like hunger, like the plague, like war.
At times my verses were embarrassingly
foolish.

But I make no excuse.
I believe that seeking beautiful words
is better
than killing and murdering.

translated by Ewald Osers

In Lenin's Mausoleum

Beneath the red wall, beneath the domes
golden and gleaming
on his catafalque in sweet repose,
as if just dreaming.

in a glass coffin Lenin lies,
as though by Death unmarred,
watching with half-closed eyes
the soldier who stands on guard.

Bayonet fixed, he passes long hours
by Lenin's side,
inhaling the scent of faded flowers
while the clock outside

marks time's swift evolution.
The red flag's still there
but where is the revolution —
where?

The Kremlin's wall, red like a field of poppies,
its teeth bares in ire.
There Comrade Stalin has his office,
but no revolutionary fire.

Suddenly the silence is shattered
by the sound of shooting —
at the Lubyanka enemies and traitors
they're executing.

Spirits of the Age

Now Lenin seems to awaken.
He stretches out a hand:
'Why do I lie here forsaken?
Tell me that, my friend.'

'When out there in the streets they need me
I cannot stay.
Don't leave me here to sleep, but lead me
to join the fray.'

But the soldier shook his head and pressed
the lid down tight.
'No, you just lie here quietly and rest.
Why go fight?'

'Sleep, comrade, and be glad you're here.
These days it's best to keep
your nose clean, don't you interfere.
Good night, go back to sleep.'

Lenin falls asleep. In his quiet tomb
the shadows gather in,
his tranquil face permeated
with wax and paraffin.

translated by George Theiner

VLADIMIR HOLAN   *Czechoslovak Socialist Republic*

About Poetry

You know not where the road starts
which will lead you nowhere.
How little you care, yet it was full of magic,
women, miracles, and a longing for freedom.
You saw how the horse seemed to be killed under
    the angel,
the angel went on foot, that's the path of self-
    abnegation,
only then did you discover human suffering,
but also divine, the God who seeks happiness,
the unhappy, loving God.

from the collection Lamento, *1970*

JAN ZAHRANDNCEK *Czechoslovak Socialist Republic*

Letter to My Wife

You talk and reminisce.
You don't know where I am, nor can you imagine
how I sit here, empty-handed,
a guest of unkind malice,
to whom the sun has become a stranger
and who, like Dante in his hell,
will for a long time not see the stars,
nor the moon, nor wind, nor your summery smile.

You don't know where I am, and yet I'm so near
I can almost hear you as you walk
silently past all those familiar objects
so as not to wake the children. It's early
and the sun is catching fire.

That great vacation sun, the harvest sun,
thunders in the streets, and here in my cell
it is as if
everyone out there was hurrying to a feast.
Why else should they sound so excited and in such haste
that all the pavements seem to sing. I can hear the
    spring in their step,
their impatience,
as if they believed their children's dreams
and were rushing to see
the unheard of miracle.

You too are out there, somewhere. Going to church
and then to the shops. You worry about the kids.
Many a revelation have you gained from them.
Many miracles you can confirm.
You believe them all,
you remember them and would like to share them with me,
if only I were back.

It all worries
my little son, you say.
Comfort him, dear, do not cry. The days are growing
    shorter.
The time of decision draws near, whatever befalls.
And remember, we are not alone. Remember the ruins
of so many homes, scattered, all those fag-ends
    flickering and fading.
It would not do to be happy
while God suffers, and the image of Man
has been defiled.

from the collection House of Fear, *1982*

Ancient Myth

In the end, it seems,
the sun always makes the same mistake
as his father, who built the labyrinth
in which he imprisoned himself. And his wings
made of the feathers and wax of dreams are too heavy
for his passion, the sun of freedom
too fierce, the steep longing
only a wall, only a maze,
and a fall will only save him
from the double-edged axe. How to seize,
he says to himself as he falls, and not to hurt yourself.
And at the very bottom of the night he sees a woman
made of foam, a reddish lap, a ribbon of blood
with which it all began and all will end.

from the collection Sentences, *1977 (samizdat)*

Homeland

Not meadows deluged with water
snow melted before its time,
not roads lined with rowan-trees
swaying in the breeze,
not railway shacks,
black mud, clay and clinkers
congealed on the passengers shoes
as they alight
and then, hunched under their invisible burdens,
disperse over the fields
towards the hamlets and cottages
you cannot see . . .

But a man, collar turned up,
all grey and grizzled now,
gazing with barren eyes
under his old hat, alone, leaning on a post,
sodden galoshes on the threshold
of a waiting-room, three walls made of planks;
a thread holding his fate
within the circle of those few dozen
muddy miles of his district
leading him, a donkey on the shaft of a treadmill,
from one station to another,
from one waiting-room to the next,
from one grey and grizzled hair
to that dirty snowdrift
which yet did not quench
something glowing in his barren look.

Not homesteads with black roofs and gates
high on the hills like so many castles,
not strings of gentle alders
along all the watery and dried-up ditches,
not the bare red bricks of housefronts
emerging from the distant fog
together with the banner of a lone green pine.

But a fellow
opening his notebook with calloused fingers
to show his boy companion
a red exotic stamp
and silently turning his head to the child
until the boy in joyful silent wonder
looks up at him.

Not a square with plague column,
with dried-up baroque fountains,
not barren streets
paved with cobblestones
on which clattered the hoops of our childhood,
not the absolute sky
of some far-off July days.

But cowsheds shining
in the night with opaque lamp
under which a milk-maid presses
her soiled head-scarf to the cow's white flank,
but a pair of silent oxen
following you in the darkness,
their split hooves
pattering in the dust of the road.

Not a country
but an image.

translated by George Theiner

IVA KOTRLA *Czechoslovak Socialist Republic*

Under the Skin

Memories collect
like books laid on top of another
in a second-hand bookshop

So I think of love
I look
partly through your eyes

What will you tell me
when you are alone

The moon was motionless
reminding me of desire

That is no sin there are others
which have a name

At Moments of Piety

That lonely cross on Golgotha —
    A periscope
through which the Earth observes us.
Out of its dust
    we're dust shedding tears
in adult unhappiness
when the Son in the arms of his
    Mother
is the only password
opening the gates of Paradise . . .

Growing Up

In the years
when the secret police
took down our faces
   as we left the church
we reached out
   into our dreams

Every evening
adulthood came, with a lamp,
to our bedside,
   quietly drew aside the curtains
and spoke to us
   gently, like a mother.

ALAIDE FOPPA *Republic of Guatemala*

Time

I

Time
is it forgetting
or the vague remembrance
of an unfinished story?
Is it losing
or that little
not swept away
by the muddy river?
Time
weaves its tapestry
and every day
unpicks it.
It is a patient devourer
wasting desire
slowly squeezing out
hope
and if one day
we finally attain
what we seemed to want
for so long
has time tirelessly
been undermining
all our expectations
we are left
with a charmless meeting
between a desire

sucked hollow
by time
and something that time
has made unrecognisable

VI

Is it from asking
too much
of time?
From having wanted to
broaden, compress
exhaust, multiply
time?
From not having known
to respect its limits?
From the absurd hope
of rescuing
lost time?
Is that why
this weariness
every day?

IX

Is the time of our dreams
time?
Or is it just the dream
of time
which consoles us
for a moment?

X

Time
leaves no wounds
leaves only absence
and forgetting.
Tears
leave no tracks
leave only a wellspring
empty.
Time
wiping away
what was about to be done
only yesterday.
Tears
waiting for another source
they can plunder
they can see dried up
by time.

XI

We live
in the act of forgetting.
We forget more
than keys
handkerchiefs
letters
appointments,
we also forget
the secret,
we also lose the past
unsuspecting.

Words

I

A childhood
fed on silence.
a youth
sown with farewells.
a life
begetting absences.
Only in words
can I hope
for presence at last.

II

I expect almost everything
from words
without even knowing
what it is they offer me
what it is they deny me
what it is beyond
the echo they arouse.
I do not know
if they are born on my lips
or if someone
is dictating them to me
in a sign language
to which I've lost the key.

VI

A whole life
searching for words
adequate
sincere
brand new
forgotten
clean.
to say
without saying
a secret that hurts.
to allow
the wound to bleed.
a comfort for
not doing
what cannot be done.

IX

Unformed words
seek their way.
They know not
where they are destined
nor towards whom.
But if they succeed
in crossing my night
of a sudden
I see them flash.

XV

It is not the words
which speak;
they say very little.
deceive.
Behind them
perhaps
a hidden voice
sometimes whispers
and with those same
well-worn words
astounds us.

XVII

Today they are no use to me
words:
they only serve
for what is already known.
Useless slavery,
if the word is lacking
for what is never said.

XIX

I shall have to learn
another language
for me to find
through silence
that lost word.
I shall have to wait.
repentant of my words,
for that unknown voice
betrothed
to jealous silence.

translated by Nick Caistor

The Heart

They say it is the size
of my clenched fist.
Small then
but enough
to set all this
in motion.
A laborer
who works hard
though longing for rest,
a prisoner
waiting in vague hope
of escape.

ARMANDO VALLADARES *Republic of Cuba*

Planted in My Chair

I am planted in my wheelchair
with the impotence of a tree
of deep roots
that let me open
my arms into branches
but don't let me
walk in the roads
of the forests that call me.
This horizon of reeds and rocks tortures me
and the blue bevy
of yellow butterflies
that I want to reach
beyond these prison bars
where the Sun belongs to everyone
with the pain and trembling of these arm-branches
where the blood-sap burns
stretched toward the impossible
in an absurd effort
while my root-feet
dry up . . . and fuse
with the iron
of my wheelchair
I am almost a tree
but a sad tree
What impotence
to be unable to run

Wings Will Grow One Day

Wings will grow some day
on my wheelchair
I will be able to fly over parks
carpeted with children and violets.

My chair will be a winged dream
without the deranging obsession of bars
and I will be able to climb the rainbow
and alight on a quiet mountain

My chair will be a dream without eyes
a metal swallow above the earth.

Christmas

It's Christmas and I'm cold
the frozen wind sinks into my bones
like a bayonet.
The gate in the back
open
is like a hole
in my back
that freezes my lungs.
It's Christmas and I'm hungry
they brought us our SUPPER
very early:
boiled macaroni
and nauseating gravy
cold
as the wind in your bones
It's Christmas and I'm sick
pain without medicine
tortures me
more than the wind
It's Christmas and I'm sleepy
I need to rest
and they prevent me —
the cold
the hunger
the coughing
It's Christmas
and only my heart is warm.

Situation

You who can choose
the direction of your footsteps
who can sink your feet
into the fresh sand
of any beach in the world
who don't know tortures
and anguishing incommunication
and deranging wire fences
You who can cast your gate
on every road
on the mountains and the rivers
on the deep forests
of butterflies and doves
without grey walls
stopping your glances.

You who can run
with your sons or brothers
wander all along the parks
with lovers and friends
beneath the eternal trees

You who forget
or don't know
that men and women
are dying
without todays or tomorrows
who can only look above
at a patch of sky sometimes.
You don't know the envy
I feel for them
              — my companions —
who at least can take a step
at the bottom of this concrete pit.

Over the Wires

Over the wives of the patio
the grey sky
and an automatic rifle
                        Soviet-made
showing off the tuft of its bayonet.
Ten cement steps
and the bars of my ward.

The Sun red
like dawn's fusillade
like a bloody flag:
everyone watches wordless
My companions say
that a cloud was approaching the Sun
that it was already getting lost below the wires
everyone came up to the bars
to follow its descent
I remained below
as if at the bottom of a hole
locked in my wheelchair
I could not come up to the bars
I felt closed in infinite night
with the sun sunken into my legs
and the evening suffocated in my wheels.

from Desde mi silla de ruedas, *1976*

JORGE VALLS ARANGO *Republic of Cuba*

Something

Something nearby
part of one
like the dough of the same bread
music of the same chord
(in the furtive dusk).

Perfume of the woods,
and the sword of the archangel
on the scarp of a cliff.
Something like a name
spoken with fragrance on the tongue
and a hidden warmth in the blood.

A cave,
with a burning light
and a young fawn
averting its eyes.

The root of a tree
where the owl nests
and the wild lilac
shyly sprouts.

A tiny bud of tenderness
that reached me in a white bird's feather.
on a cloistered day
of covered mirrors.

Spirits of the Age

Like a hand touching one's breast
that spreads and opens
dispensing songs of praise;
like the feet of the weightless wayfarer.
Something like that;
don't you agree?

Like a Wounded Beast

lying in the dust
licking the crusty stones,
kissing them till my gums hurt,
lifting up my flank
amid the surly bramble bushes,
gnawing on hard stalks
and devouring insects,
seeking a sharp nail
into which to drive my chest
With eyelids swollen from pouring myself out,
mingled in the smells of the earth.
Like a mangy dog and a useless weed,
musicked by all the words you utter,
your fingers clasping my ears
and holding up my face with shuttered eyes,
feeling my blood with its impurities,
acid and roiling,
which are of no consequence to your love,
clothed in the skins you bring,
adoring your scolding,
adoring the thrashing,
adoring your pestering hand,
detached,
dried to a crisp on the bleached soil,
criss-crossed
like a hill by my own footsteps,
hearing your tempestuous roar,
the fire igniting my eyes,
feeling the flames at my back
oh so intense, disjointed,
like earth, like water,
like breath so much your own, recovered.

Why Have You Left Me in the Pits So Dark?

I've been bitten by the vipers.
They've torn my flesh and spat on me,
smeared my mouth with filth
and delivered me to stinking sour smells.
I heard the laughter of the snakes,
scorning me; the contempt
of the foulest creatures.
I was sick of myself; a hundred times I was struck
by the hard tombstones;
a hundred times they covered me
with burning oils.
My eyes had no filters of sin,
nor did the acid of evil spells
twitch in my bone marrow.
You let me weaken: my fragile leg
twisted like a reed, my throat
opening up into wails, jaws gaping,
and I did what I did not want to do.
There was no vulture's skin
to cover my nakedness,
and all the shame of seeing myself,
through hidden moons, spilled into the night.
Muddied, oily, covered with dung;
eyes without tears, impure, deceased,
purchasers of death, swollen belly,
shameless lip gaping in supplication.
While the jailed wolves drooled,
their fierce jaws ajar.
Who'll pick up my rotting extremities?
Who'll open up my coffer of worms
and gather up my viscous fluids?

Who'll purify the gaze from my eyes
and relax my grim, twisted hands?
Who'll wash a pitiless groin
and make the rivers flow
over the smoking ashes?
Who'll revive a dead log?
O water, cover me, turn me over, wash me;
O water, find me, let me emerge.
Blood-water, blood-water, pooled water.

Burn, Wilderness, in Hidden Embers

My face pounds
through the silence's hard stoning,
parched as a floor at high noon,
flayed by fever,
with the last tremors
undoing my viscera
my eyes bulging till they pang with pain
and my veins thrashed by blood,
stretched like rubber bands.
I, who no longer am,
and no longer care,
(for it isn't right to make so much of self
when there's someone else who cries out unknowingly),
blown away by a double flight
of light and shadow,
braided thus in a single root.
Quickly into nothingness;
sterile even for poetry,
waiting for you.
oh, waiting.

I Am Up to My Neck in Rising Blood

It's a black and sour blood.
I am tied up with a rope of blood.
I'm speaking with a voice
made of bubbles of blood.
I'm being heard by five ears of blood.
I'm travelling in a blood-smeared car.
I'm disintegrating into worms of blood.
The worms grow and multiply
(it is the destiny of blood).
They are invading everything.
They are sputtering like clay rattles:
. . . Abel . . . Abel . . . Abel . . .
A hundred skulls are served up in blood
upon a bare table.
I'm talking, unwittingly, with the creator of the blood,
with the bestower of the blood.
The blood reaches my nostrils.
The whole world is sinking in a vomit of blood.
. . . Abel . . . Abel . . . Abel . . .

Where I Am There Is No Light

and it is barred.
Just beyond
there lies a lighted space.
Therefore light must exist.
Nonetheless,
further on, there is an even deeper gloom.
There are no hanged men now:
all of them are on fire.[1]
Could they be made of kerosene inside?
They go on talking,
moving from here to there,
from there to here,
Unendingly.
Some are sleeping.
Someone is outside.
Somewhere there is sunshine.
Inevitably, the sun exists.
I can no longer leave:
I'll go and sleep.
Inevitably, I'll wake up again.
And so on, and on and on.
The kerosene burns inexhaustibly.[2]

[1] A reference to the torturing of prisoners.
[2] The torturing goes on.

My Face

My face is a wall.
I sprinkle it with talc, I wash it;
I leave it to die furrowed by beetles.
It is still a wall.

My face is a nothingness
built from a lack of looks
from the incoherent language
with which we tear each other,
smoke, the flight of a fly.

My face is a stone.

When my face is of water
smiles great me like birds.
But the water goes by
and my face becomes of air
which only the torn leaves know . . .
as they fall to the dust.
My face is a hole
I cannot tear off.

MAURICIO ROSENCOF *Oriental Republic of Uruguay*

My dockyard sends you this boat, love
it's made of paper
no hard-keeled ships
no sharp-prowed sailing ships
are left
Just a little paper boat, love
and this unbounded
will
to voyage once again

*

Do you know, little daughter
dreams
wander strangely
in the small hours they slip away
in smokey pirouettes
through windows
they flutter, they live
nibble at crumbs, drink in water tanks
are threadlets of cotton
vagabonds of the spring

They covered the light
censored the windows
Voice was dissolved
Everything was nothing
But they were there
Outside
They were there

*

Fingers
Caressed
The dark shreds
And the cigarette
Nested in the little paper
It was in the darkness
Of the lavatory
And squatting
The first
Tepid
Clandestine puff

translated by Malcolm Coad

MAURICIO REDOLES *Republic of Chile*

Press Conference

"In Chile there are no political prisoners
The ones there are are
politicians who are prisoners
are
Prisoners who are not political
just
prisoners"
Since when do we have to
explain so many things?
   (the general perspires)

"Here we've put an end to Marxism
There are no more social classes
They were abolished the
proletariat was dissolved through proclamation
Number twenty whatever"
   (the general smiles)

"No, no, no
Our economic policies
Benefit no one
Here we all have to tighten our belts we
are all equal
Yes
There is unemployment, hunger, but . . ."

"No, no, no, no," I said, "it rankles
   unemployment, it rankles"
you get that?

"Yes
Put that down yes
put it down and send it to the embassy"
    (the general sighs)

"The disappeared?
There have always been disappeared people in Chile
For example Lieutenant Bello in the illustrious history . . .
In the history of our . . .
In the air force . . .
Lieutenant Bello, for example
You understand?"
    (the general looks at his adviser slyly)

"Freedom of the press yes
Yes there is freedom of the press any
Person who does not contravene our norms
Has the right to publish whatever
He wishes but
He'd better respect our arms . . .
    I mean norms"
    (the general has lost his color)

translated by John Lyons

[Lieutenant Bello was a 1920s Chilean Air Force pilot who disappeared while trying to fly over the Andes to Argentina. His fate has given rise to a popular expression in Chile: "to be as lost as Lieutenant Bello."]

The Future Will Return

The future will return
with a certainty of fire and stone
with a precision of spiders and rain

Leading sailor Ernesto Zuñiga
will again run half-naked from his cell
towards the showers
in Valparaiso Public Jail

Alicia Rios will again turn a corner
close to Finsbury Park, London, N.4

before dying blown to pieces
on a street in Santiago

The future will return
stubborn as a root, as bone
immaculate as the entire earth

The future will return
with the death of its young
vanquished through its surprise

restored to its plain
vulgarity it will travel by our side

when the future returns

sharp as a cricket singing

accurate

in the silence/in the night of light

translated by John Lyons

Otters

to Luis Castelgrande,
nearly a hunter of otters

Otters don't kill each other in ottercide wars
Otters don't drink alcohol, just a drop of water
Otters don't smoke or take drugs

Otters dress themselves in their own skin
It would never occur to an otter to kill a human being
In order to make a human overcoat for itself

Otters don't fall asleep watching television
Otters don't make films

Otters don't torture other otters nor make them disappear

They don't have the technology or the
intelligence to be able to do it

Otters don't play rugby or buy shares

Otters don't have any class struggle
Otters don't divide themselves up into social classes
Otters don't live on the surplus value
produced by other otters

Otters don't drive motorized vehicles
Nor do they punish the planet

Otters cannot unleash the nuclear holocaust

At the most a squabble between a
mother otter jealous of her puppy otters

And a resentful father otter

On the shores of Lake Ofqui in South America
Or on a beach in the north of Scotland

But nothing in the way of nuclear holocausts

They don't have the technology nor the
intelligence to be able to do it

translated by John Lyons

ROQUE DALTON *Republic of El Salvador*

Jail again, dark fruit.

In the streets and rooms of men, someone at this moment will be moaning in love, will be making music or reading news of a battle happening under the Asian night. In the rivers, fishes will sing of their disbelief in the sea, impossible dream, too good to be true. (I speak of those fish, in reality blue, called Lily-Blacks, from whose spines violent and swift men extract perfumes of great durability.)

And, in whatever place, the least of sunken or nailed down things will be less prisoner than I.

(True, my having a piece of pencil and paper — and poetry — proves that some puffed-up universal concept, born to be written in capitals — Truth, God, The Unknown — flooded me one happy day, and that I have not fallen — fallen into this dark well — but into the hands of opportunity in order to give proper evidence of it before mankind.

Nevertheless, I would prefer a walk in the country.

Even without a dog.)

translated by Tim Reynolds

Some Nostalgias

Horny privilege this proud suffering, don't laugh.

I, who have loved until thirsty for water, dingy light;
I who forgot the names and not the wetness
now would die fiercely for a small word of consolation
    from an angel
for the singable talents of an unhappy bat
for the magic bread thrown to me by a warlock
disguised as a drunken criminal in the next cell . . . .

translated by Tim Reynolds

At the Bottom

Country of mine you don't exist
you are only my poor silhouette
a word I believed from the enemy

Before I thought it was just you were very small
you didn't manage to have at once
North and South
but now I know you don't exist
and besides it seems no one needs you
one doesn't hear any mother speak of you

That makes me happy
because it proves I've invented a country
though I might then owe myself to the asylums

I am therefore a little god at your expense

(What I mean is: me being expatriated
you are ex patria)

translated by Tim Reynolds

Bad News on a Scrap of Newspaper

These days when friends of mine die
only their names die.

How can one hope, from this violent well,
to reach more than the newsprint,
its splendour of delicate blacks,
arrows in our deepest memories?
Only those who live outside prisons
can honour the corpses, wash off
the pain of their dead with embraces
scratch with tear and nail at tombstones.

Prisoners cannot: we simply whistle
hoping the echo will silence the news.

JAVIER HERAUD   *Republic of Peru*

The Art of Poetry

Really, to speak of it really,
poetry is hard work that wins or loses
on the beat of autumnal years.

(When you're young
& the fallen flowers are never picked again
you write and write between nightfalls,
and hundreds and hundreds, sometimes, of useless
pages get filled.
You can brag and say:
"I write, I don't amend,
poems fall from my hand like the spring
they cut down the old cypresses in my street")
But time passes agreeably, and
the years line up between the brows,
poetry goes on becoming
pottery,
   clay that bakes between the hands,
   clay that brisk fires shape.
And poetry is a
marvelous flash of light,
a rain of silent words,
a wood full of throbbing and hope,
the songs of oppressed peoples,
the new song of liberated peoples.

And poetry is, then,
love and death,
the restoration of man.

Madrid 1961 — Havana 1962

translated by Paul Blackburn

Word of the Guerrilla Fighter

Because my country is fair
as a sword in air
and greater now, even,
and fairer still, I
speak and I defend her
with my life.
Traitors? What
do I care what they say, we
have closed the pass
with bulky tears
of steel.
The sky is ours.
Ours the daily bread, we
have sowed and reaped
the wheat and the earth,
they are ours, and ours
forever are
the sea,
the mountains,
and the birds.

translated by Paul Blackburn

CLARIBEL ALEGRIA *Republic of El Salvador*

Personal Data

I am five feet five.
I have brown eyes.
Do I dare to laugh,
to ask,
to destroy the armour they place
over me or to cry ashamed?
I know how to read and write
but I am unable to forget my rancour.
I have never been in prison.
Why so many marks against me
if it is so difficult to know one another?
During the night I argue with my thoughts,
In my dreams I disguise myself.
A number identifies me and I choke with thirst.
But despite everything the singing lifts from me
And they don't know what to do about this at Customs
except to allow it to pass through.

Dream

I dreamt
that I was a wing
I awoke
with a tugging
at my roots.

Everything Is Normal in Our Backyard

And in spite of the sun
the air
the doves
the inquisitor goes on
tending his roses
removes weeds
stones
gnarled roots
he turns the earth
looks again
keeps off
the marchioness
as always at her crochet-work
every time someone goes by
her glasses fall off
slight shifts in tone
to indicate rank
the lonely man dances
longing to smash his shadow
into a thousand pieces
the one they crucified
is getting old
no-one listens anymore
to his prophecies
the iconoclastic
clown goes over to him
and places in his mouth
a cigarette

have a drag boss
have a drag
but he spits it out
and the squatting beggar
picks it up
the clouds shimmer
a fragrance of jasmine rises
along the walls
the jailer
walks by dressed in white
looks for his friend
the priest
the hangman has arrived
and it is time
check
declares the general
his partner starts
with fright
he blocks it with his bishop
mate
the general fires
and the victim
topples headlong
I leave the inquisitor
crushing insects
everything is normal
in our backyard
with fists
feet saliva
two guys are fighting

one wants
the other to tell him
he knows that he knows
he does not know
nor does the other
the psychiatrist leans over
I try hard not to say
Old man God
which of them is right?
I do say it
I make a point of it
I wait
he smiles
and asks:
How are your verses
coming along?

Mortally Wounded

When I woke up
this morning
I knew you were
mortally wounded
that I was too
that our days were counted
our nights
that someone had counted them
without letting us know
that more than ever
I had to love you
you had to love me.
I inhaled your fragrance
I watched you sleeping
I ran the tips of my fingers
over your skin
remembered the friends
whose quota was filled
and are on the other side:
the one who died
a natural death
the one who fell in combat
the one they tortured
in jail
who kicked aside his death.
I brushed your warmth
with my lips:

mortally wounded
my love
perhaps tomorrow
and I loved you more than ever
and you loved me as well.

translated by Caroline Forché

JUAN GELMAN *Argentine Republic*

Deeds

I would like to know
what I am doing here under this roof safe
from the cold the heat I mean
what am I doing
while el Comandante Segundo other men
are hounded to death
are returned to the air to kingdom come
and sadness and pain have names
and there are shots in the night and you can't sleep.

translated by Janet Brof

[Ricardo Jorge Masetti, a noted Argentine journalist who organized the People's Guerrilla Army, was imprisoned and tortured and died at the age of 35. He was called El Comandante Segundo; Che Guevara was to become El Comandante Primero.]

Exile

I love this foreign land for what it gives
me, and for what it cannot give me.

Because my land is unique. It is not the
best, it is unique. Foreigners can respect it
without loving it because they, being
different, are in a different way beautiful.

I am touched by their beauties. But their
way of reaching beauty is not mine.

This is moving: in offering me their
beauty, they also show me the foreignness
of that beauty. Almost always, injustice,
pain, suffering get in the way.

Here's to you, beauty. All of us are
fragments in the universal voyage, different,
opposites, yet the same waves lift us on.

We will fall together on a shore
somewhere. We'll build a fire against the
cold and hunger.

We will burn under the same night.

We will see each other, see.

Rome, 1980.

The Game We Play

If they'd let me, I'd choose
this wholesomeness of being quite sick
this happiness of going on very unhappy.

If they'd let me, I'd choose
this innocence of not being an innocent
this purity through which I pass for impure.

If they'd let me, I'd choose
this love with which I hate
this hope which eats desperate bread.

There you have it, gentlemen
I toss my life on the table.

translated by Janet Brof

Victory

In a book of verses splashed
with love, with sadness, with the world,
my children drew yellow women,
elephants advancing over red umbrellas,
birds held back at the edge of a page,
they invaded death,
the huge blue camel rests on a sooty word,
a cheek slides along the solitude of my bones,
candor wins over the jumble of the night.

translated by Janet Brof

JUAN FRANCISCO GUTIERREZ   *Republic of Nicaragua*

Death of the Guerrilla

For conquering Liberty, the warrior died.
Today his name echoes in the memory of his people!
We choose words to fight for our freedom.
In his name they beat us even beneath our tongues.
He loved unclaimed land, now he has plenty of dark earth.
The poppies tread on his scattered bones.
In the hostile territory burned by the heart,
he helped us advance. Prisoner of death, left
like an eternal blow against the door of our delay,
his name is a new song we hear at night.

Requiem for the Dead Poets of My Country

They wrote poems in the night, and they loved.
They didn't try to replace any god
or to impose beauty and lordliness. In their hearts
they carried the burning cipher: Nicaragua.
That's exactly where they kept her, always
surrounding her with love beneath the moon.
And that's enough. Salomn, Joaquin: against
the sunset your faces remain. Rubén said once
that magic nightingales sang in his eyes of water.
Azaharìas saw roads without answers
and Manolo walked down them three times, in exile.
Death has cut their blue tendons, but
the salt of the earth sprouts from those closed eyes.

MAHMUD DARWISH *State of Israel (Palestine)*

The Roses and the Dictionary

Be that as it may,
I must . . .
the poet must have a new toast
And new anthems.
Traversing a tunnel of incense
And pepper and ancient summer,
I carried the key to legends and ruined monuments of slaves.
I see history an old man
Tossing dice and gathering the stars.

Be that as it may,
I must refuse death
Even though my legends die.
In the rubble I rummage for light and new poetry.
Did you realize before today, my love,
That a letter in the dictionary is dull?
How do they live, all these words?
How do they grow? How do they spread?
We still water them with the tears of memories
And metaphors and sugar.
Be that as it may,
I must reject the roses that spring
From a dictionary or a *diwan*.[1]
Roses grow on the arms of a peasant, on the fists of a laborer,
Roses grow over the wounds of a warrior
And on the face of a rock.

---

[1] A diwan *is a collection of poems by a single author.*

A Lover from Palestine

Your eyes are a thorn in my heart
Inflicting pain, yet I cherish that thorn
And shield it from the wind.
I sheathe it in my flesh, I sheathe it, protecting it from
    night and agony,
And its wound lights the lanterns,
Its tomorrow makes my present
Dearer to me than my soul.
And soon I forget, as eye meets eye,
That once, behind the doors, there were two of us.

Your words were a song
And I tried to sing, too.
But agony encircled the lips of spring.
and like the swallow, your words took wing,
The door of our home and the autumnal threshold migrated,
To follow you wherever led by longing.
Our mirrors were shattered,
And sorrow was multiplied a thousandfold.
And we gathered the splinters of sound,
Mastering only the elegy of our homeland!
Together we will plant it in the heart of a lyre,
and on the rooftops of our tragedy we'll play it
To mutilated moons and to stones.
But I have forgotten, you of the unknown voice:
Was it your departure that rusted the lyre or was it my silence?

Yesterday I saw you in the port,
A lone voyager without provisions,
Like an orphan I ran to you,
Asking the wisdom of our forefathers:
How can the ever-verdant orange grove be dragged
To prison, to exile, to a port,
And despite all her travels,
Despite the scent of salt and longing,
Remain ever green?
I write in my diary:
I love oranges and hate the port.
And I write further:
On the dock
I stood, and saw the world through winter's eyes.
Only the orange peel is ours, and behind me lay the desert.

In the briar-covered mountains I saw you,
A shepherdess without sheep,
Pursued among the ruins.
You were my garden, and I a stranger,
Knocking at the door, my heart,
For upon my heart stand firm
The door and windows, the cement and stones.

I have seen you in casks of water, in granaries,
Broken, I have seen you a maid in night clubs,
I have seen you in the gleam of tears and in wounds.
You are the other lung in my chest;
You are the sound on my lips;
You are water, you are fire.

Poets of Conscience

I saw you at the mouth of the cave, at the cavern,
Hanging your orphans' rags on the washline.
In the stoves, in the streets I have seen you.
In the barns and in the sun's blood.
In the songs of the orphaned and the wretched I have seen you.
I have seen you in the salt of the sea and in the sand
Yours was the beauty of the earth, of children and of Arabian
  jasmine.

And I have vowed
To fashion from my eyelashes a kerchief,
And upon it to embroider verses for your eyes,
And a name, when watered by a heart that dissolves in
chanting,
Will make the sylvan arbors grow.
I shall write a phrase more precious than honey and kisses:
"Palestinian she was and still is."

On a night of storms, I opened the door and the window
To see the hardened moon of our nights.
I said to the night: Run out,
Beyond the darkness and the wall;
I have a promise to keep with words and light.
You are my virgin garden
As long as our songs
Are swords when we draw them.
And you are as faithful as grain
So long as our songs
Keep alive the fertile soil when we plant them.
You are like a palm tree in the mind:
Neither storm nor woodsman's ax can fell it.

Spirits of the Age

Its braids uncut
By the beasts of desert and forest.
But I am the exiled one behind wall and door,
Shelter me in the warmth of your gaze.

Take me, wherever you are,
Take me, however you are.
To be restored to the warmth of face and body,
To the light of heart and eye,
To the salt of bread and song,
To the taste of earth and homeland.

Shelter me in the warmth of your gaze,
Take me, a panel of almond wood, in the cottage of sorrows,
Take me, a verse from the book of my tragedy,
Take me, a plaything or a stone from the house,
So that our next generation may recall
The path of return to our home.

Her eyes and the tattoo on her hands are Palestinian,
Her name, Palestinian,
Her dreams and sorrow, Palestinian,
Her kerchief, her feet and body, Palestinian,
Her words and her silence, Palestinian,
Her voice, Palestinian,
Her birth and her death, Palestinian.
I have carried you in my old notebooks
As the fire of my verses,
The sustenance of my journeys.
In your name, my voice rang in the valleys:
I have seen Byzantium's horses
Even though the battle be different.

Beware, oh beware
The lightning struck by my song in the granite.
I am the flower of youth and the knight of knights!
I am the smasher of idols.
I plant the Levantine borders
With poems that set eagles free.
And in your name I have shouted at the enemy:
Worms, feed on my flesh if ever I slumber,
For the eggs of ants cannot hatch eagles,
And the shell of the adder's egg
Holds but a snake!
I have seen Byzantium's horses,
And before it all, I know
That I am the flower of youth and the knight of knights!

Concerning Hopes

Tell me not:
  I wish I were a baker in Algeria
  That I might sing with a freedom fighter.
Tell me not:
  I wish I were a shepherd in Yemen
  That I might sing of the eruptions of time.
Tell me not:
  I wish I were a waiter in Havana
  That I might sing of the victories of the sorrowful.
Tell me not:
  I wish I were a young porter in Aswan
  That I might sing to the rocks.

My friend!
The Nile will never flow into the Volga,
Nor will the Congo or the Jordan river flow into the
Euphrates.
Each river has its own source, its course, and its life.
My friend! Our land is no barren land.
Each land is born in due time;
With every dawn, a freedom fighter rises.

RASHID HUSAYN *State of Israel (Palestine)*

To a Cloud

I am the land,
I am the land . . . do not deny me rain,
I am all that remains of it,
If you plant my brow with trees
And turn my poetry into vineyards,
   And wheat
      and roses
         That you may know me.
         So let the rain pour down.

I, cloud of my life, am the hills of Galilee,
I am the bosom of Haifa
   And the forehead of Jaffa.
   So do not whisper: it is impossible.
Can you not hear my child's approaching footsteps
   At the threshold of your soul?
Can you not see the veins of my brow
   Striving to kiss your lips?

Waiting for you, my poetry turned to earth,
   Has become fields,
   Has turned into wheat
   And trees.
I am all that remains of our earth,
I am all that remains of what you love,
   So pour . . . pour with bounty,
   Pour down the rain.

                                        Spirits of the Age

At Zero Hour

At zero hour, I phoned God a million times
Saying: Come, let us while away the evening hours!
And He was bold, replying:
I will, but to what purpose?
Why, to drink together, said I.

My God, rich and handsome, traveled aboard the most modern
planes,
Kept my closest pals tucked away in banks,
    And all the beautiful women he desired.
Geneva became his mistress,
    Her bosom adorned with conference flowers.

I wonder who has really changed,
Was it my heart or God that changed yesterday?
My story is a little girl, born between Jaffa, Haifa and my love,
    Nothing about her has changed;
I murdered the refugee camp a million times,
    Yet nothing in it has changed;
I dwelled in hotels writing verses,
    Nothing there has ever changed;
I saw the capitals of fifty diverse lands,
    And nothing in me has changed.
I traced the outlines of my country upon my heart
Turning myself into an atlas for her contours,
While she became the milk of my verse,
    Yet nothing in it has changed.
I wonder, what has really changed?
Is it my heart or God himself?
Or has everything changed?

I will go on writing, more and more,
I will go on loving, more and more,
I will even draw the flies that plagued Jaffa and Haifa,
   So that I may go on growing.
There will be ports with ships from Genoa, urging me
   To travel farther,
But I will cut all the telephone lines,
Demolish all the ports
   And turn the spring of the beast into autumn.

I will transform my life into all likelihoods of war,
   So that the seed of love within me may grow,
   and I will phone God a million times.
   I will go on singing, more and more,
   I will go on growing.

SAMIH AL-QASIM   *Arab Republic of Egypt*

A Homeland

So what,
When in my homeland
The sparrow dies of starvation,
In exile, without a shroud,
While the earthworm is satiated,
Devouring God's food!

So what,
When the yellow fields
Yield no more to their tillers
Than memories of weariness,
While their rich harvest pours
Into the granaries of the usurper!

So what,
If the cement has diverted
The ancient springs,
causing them to forget their natural course,
When their owner calls,
They cry in his face: "Who are you?"

So what,
When the almond and the olive have turned to timber
Adorning tavern doorways,
And monuments
Whose nude loveliness beautifies halls and bars,
And is carried by tourists
To the farthest corners of the earth,
while nothing remains before my eyes
But dry leaves and tinder!

So what,
When my people's tragedy
Has turned to farce in others' eyes.
And my face is a poor bargain
That even the slave-trader gleefully disdains!

So what,
When in barren space the satellites spin,
And in the streets walks a beggar, holding a hat,
And the song of autumn is heard!
Blow, East winds!
Our roots are still alive!

The Thunderbird

It surely will come,
Will come with the sun;
Its face deformed by the dust of textbooks.

It surely will come,
After the wind has died in my voice,
Something whose wonders have no bounds;
Something that is named in songs:
The Thunderbird!

It is bound to come:
For we have reached it,
We have reached the summit of death!

*[The Thunderbird is a holy symbol of freedom in the legends of the Zuni Indians,
a North American tribe.]*

AHMED FOUAD NEGM   *Arab Republic of Egypt*

Prisoner's File

Name   Sabr

Charge   That I am Egyptian.

Age   The most modern age
(though grey hair in braids flows from my head down to my waist).

Profession   Heir, of my ancestors and of time, to the creation of civilisation and life-force and peace.

Skin   Wheat-colored.

Figure   As slim as a lance.

Hair   Rougher than dried clover.

Color of eyes   Jet black.

Nose   Aquiline like a horse's.

Mouth   Firmly in place
(when I attempted to budge it, some mischief happened).

Spirits of the Age

Place of birth   In any dark room
    under the sky,
    on the soil of Egypt.
    From any house in the middle of palm trees,
    where the Nile flows —
    as long as it is not a palace.

Verdict   For seven thousand years
    I have been a prisoner asleep,
    grinding stones with my molars,
    out of frustration,
    spending the nights in grief.

The question of release   Someone asked me:
    "Why is your imprisonment so long?"

    "Because I am a peaceful and a humorous man.
    I did not break the law,
    because I am afraid of it;
    the law holds a sword in its hands.

    Anytime you want —
    ask the informers about me
    and you will hear and understand
    my story from A to Z.

My name is Sabr,
Ayyub, patient with catastrophes,
like a donkey,
I carry my share of the burden
and wait.
I drown in rivers of sweat
all day long.
At night I gather together my troubles
and upon them I lie,
do you know why?''

translated by Janet Stevens and Moussa Saker

[Sabr is a common Arabic name which means 'patience.' Ayyub is a personality in Arab folk literature known for his unending patience.]

SAEED SOLTANPOUR   *Islamic Republic of Iran*

On This Shore of Fear

No
I will reach
Heights of madness and fury
No
To the farthest blood-red star
I will soar and scale peaks of revulsion.

I will plunge down
Heights of fortitude
Into deepest stretches of the dark-stained marsh
And there I will rest
Like a water-lily anticipating my lover's anger
Shedding from my laurels the pollen of mutiny
Upon the dead water.

Consider the plain:
Menacing waters
Feeding on our love-drenched blood.
Black are the sails
Burnt out crucifixes for these graves of the sea.

Observe the martyrs riding westward
Hear the soreness of their blood-torn voices
Remember in the confusion
The fishers' seasoned nets
Catching corpses
From these muddy waters.

In the fallow ground of this silence
On this shore of fear
Upon this plain of blood roses and iron stalks
I will not stay silent.

I chose defiance
The way of those poets of the past
The way of Eshghi, the way of Farrokhi.
So hear my voice
As it sings in the slaughter-house.

Another colour covers my hoarsened voice:
Rage red ferocity of an eagle
Beating its wings at twilight on the heights.
The molten spikes of his cries
Circle and soar high over the lines
Where the future and the revolution meet.

The waves will bring me a boat
And on the sea I will remain
Sailing across to death.
But the seeds will be there
Seeds of the ever-green flower
Seeds of my being
Planted somewhere on the road
Somewhere by the house where our people live
In the feverish garden of the tulips.

After the dry spring of a defeated nation
Sow the field with mingled seeds
Hide them by the furnace
Scatter them on the land
And watch them grow in silence
Into the future rising.

translated by Patrick Cross

[Eshghi and Farrokhi, two of Iran's leading poets, also died in the struggle for freedom.]

RAAD MUSHATAT   *Islamic Republic of Iraq*

Many Dresses

On the night before this one
Her arms on my chest
as she thinks in confusion of the
five hours
she will spend in the aeroplane
alone . . .
beset by sorrow

They killed a woman in the capital
The peasant officers of the secret police

On the night before this one
I scolded her for the many dresses
which she carried in the suitcase
and the plastic shoes
too . . .

We did not have supper
There were only cigarettes
and a low temperature
that makes the wall cold
and prickly

She was not clever enough
to hide her beauty
so much that it made you smile

Oh, what an ordinary day
humid . . . and putrid
as they crushed her make-up
and lodged her in a brothel
and gave her four blankets
and a little
fear
in order to sleep
She withered away in their fingers
dangling from golden rings

Over and over they blight human beings
Over and over they blight their brains

How often does this happen
Oh, peasant officers of the secret police

Today is ordinary
and when I entered the garden
the sky was overcast
as I searched for the many dresses
and the arm on my chest

translated by Shirley Eber

Three Iraqi Women 1979

Her husband did not return from work
He entered the bus crammed
with bodies
and chattering heads
locked heads
fixed heads

He sat at the back
arranged his black jacket
took the collar of his crumpled shirt from its fold
and began to smoke a roll-up

'On the outskirts of the capital
the military police are examining the names
of comers and goers, carrying lists of
workers, college students, doctors . . .
who are communists, and arresting them . . .'

Only . . . her husband
with a black jacket
and crumpled shirt
entered the bus
and did not return

She is still young
and does not know the fascists
or understand a thing

Her husband left her his colored military photo

'When he was a soldier on compulsory service
in the northern war'
The family next door to them
were all annihilated within the rooms of their small house
and she saw the sound of the fascists' feet
behind the closed door
. . . their conceited feet

When she returned home
her three brothers were no longer there
only . . . the buttons
of their summer shirts
which they wore this morning
scattered among the furniture
and the door handle smashed
and the ends of foreign cigarettes
she had never seen before
stubbed out on the walls . . .

translated by Shirley Eber

AHMAD SHAMLOU   *Islamic Republic of Iran*

The Game Is Over

Lovers passed by, heads down
Awkward with their untimely songs

Murmurs and footsteps
Vanished from the streets

Soldiers passed by, battered and exhausted
Riding their mutilated horses
Their lowered bayonets
Smeared with bleached pride

What use flaunting your victory
to the universe
When every speck of dust
Whirls up, cursing you!

What are trees and gardens to you
When you always speak to the jasmin
With a scythe

wherever you step
The plants cease to grow
For you never had faith
In the holiness of earth and water

Alas!
Our life-story
Was the hollow song
of your troops
Returning from their conquest of a whore-house

Black shrouded mothers
Demented by the loss
Of earth's precious children
Have not yet raised their heads
From their prayer-mats
See what fate awaits you
When demonic curses will descend on you.

translated by F. Safiri

MEEM ATASH *Islamic Republic of Iran*

You Are the Singer

Do not ask me for a new song.
They have taken my voice away;
I am now only an ex-singer.
Do not ask me for a new poem.
They have stolen my rhymes and metres;
I am now only an ex-poet.
Do not ask me for a new tale.
My people are now all in prison;
I am now only an ex-story teller.
Do not ask me for a new lesson.
They have driven me out of my school-house
Turning it into a sordid temple
In honor of their resurgent Baal.
Today, I am only an ex-teacher.
You who are fighting on the side of life
By retrieving our yesterdays
And imagining our tomorrows —
Today, you are the one who sings the song,
Writes the poem, tells the story,
Teaches the lesson that we all need
To be singers, poets, writers
And teachers of freedom.

translated by Amir Taheri

Spirits of the Age

ABDELLATIF LAABI *Kingdom of Morocco*

They Came Looking for You

One day
they came looking for you
for you too
They couldn't forgive you
for being the companion
of a rebel poet
for loving an outcast
and for sustaining him with your own
resistance
You knew
the night of the blindfold
the underworld of the Question
you heard those voices
beyond humanity
shouting words of menace and sarcasm
you felt before you
those tatty men (so little like men)
whom you knew were torturers and assassins
you felt near you
other men (a little more than ordinary men)
scarred by electrodes and whips
but with unwavering hearts
And so
there is nothing left to hide from you

Heresy

Have you heard about
my latest heresy
You won't believe me
but it is that
I sing of the happiness of love

The Poem Beneath the Gag (I)

Hello sun of my country
how good it is to be alive today
so much light around me
Hello waste ground of my walks
I've got to know you
I walk across you at a brisk pace
and you suit me like an elegant old shoe
Hello wise old clumsy pecker bird
perched up there
on the wall which hides the world from me
distractedly
ruffling your feathers
Hello stunted alley grass
rustling in shimmering ripples
beneath the wind's teasing caress
Hello solitary palm tree
tall and straight
but like a splendid open flower
at your top
Hello sun of my country
your tidal presence wipes out exile
so much light so much light around me

I have a thousand reasons to live
to conquer daily death
to know the happiness of loving you
to keep in step with hope

All is not for the best
throughout the world
'comrades' kill each other
the yanks play at being referees
the road is long for the world's peoples
who more than ever must
rely on themselves

'We need all our wits'
to face failure
disillusion
obstinate facts which corrode
naïve dreams
and this new lucidity makes
the road shorter

To learn silence
so that our words weigh
their full weight of suffering
to express our quintessential acts
beneath the executioner's blindfold
to know how to identify the blindfold
of our own pride

Struggling with time
memory
ebbs and flows
there is no present
unless you call present
this acute awareness
of the future
striking down the past

So many years
not to have known
loneliness or boredom
so many shooting stars inside my head
the fountain of tenderness murmurs
insistently
the strange happiness of the prisoner

The night has unleashed its horde of doves
upon the sensual forests of remembrance
you appear before me
terrifying full of feminine charm and promise
and then comes the ritual
punctuated by explosions
by guffawing voyeurs in their stinking hoods
I am but half a man

The water flows through my fingers
iridescent droplets
absorb the sun greedily
to dream is only the reflection
of the near miracle

The smile dawns by itself
I don't wipe it from my face
my forgotten face and all mirrors
irrepressible smile
this is how I resist

The comrades sleep
the prison has stopped spinning round their heads
they sail with open hearts
in the high sea of our uncensored passions
They are beautiful in their sleep

every day
there's this white sheet of paper which defies me
as if to decree the victory of silence
a thousand poems shattered under the daily debris
perverse time unreeling the words to express them

You've got it wrong Comrades
Wrong Wrong Wrong
I do not want to believe in your hands
your hands of exemplary craftsmen
   pillaging hope
(playing with the lives of the children of
the new world)
Peace on Ho Chi Minh
Peace on Phnom Penh
Peace on your hands

(January 8, 1978)

translation by Ariel Daigré

MANG KE *People's Republic of China*

III

Here it is blackest night
walls on four sides
only above your head is there no roof
Above your head is a tapestry woven
    of the starlit sky
You often use it, when crying
to wipe the tears from your face
Here it is blackest night
this black night imprisons you within
    its walls
Frequently, on the edge of sleep, you
struggle to be free of the walls' rough
    arms
imploring the Heavens
Ah, the Heavens, the most she can give
    you
are those eyes fixed upon you.

XVI

On the windowpane of your open eyes
I see the night
its full, dense beard
nestled against your face
this moment you are terrified
Why do you still not sleep?
Whom do you await?
this moment suddenly the moon's
    sharp tongue
tears apart the layers of cloud
in a twinkling, I saw you smile
before your eyes, I see
that radiance reappear
like the beating of a white dove's wings
circling outside your window.

XXIII

Land, my aged land
you have watched me grow from
    childhood, but now
when that merciless, setting sun
moves to drag me, as if its own
    radiance from your breast
How can my heart be so hard as
    to cast you aside
How can I bear in the dark to
    hear you cry
raised by your hands, to you I owe
    my heart
though thereafter my body ceases
    to exist
I still want to give you my soul
Have faith in me, my Land
should one day while still asleep
you hear Light's hand knock at
    your door
that could announce my return
Please, for my sake, for the
    coming of such light,
open your large door wide.

from Jiumeng, *(Old Dream), 1980*
translated by Elizabeth Rogers

Spirits of the Age

KIM KWANGSOP   *Democratic People's Republic of Korea*

The Pigeons of Songbukdong

Songbuk Hill has changed its address,
but only the pigeons who lived there forever
have lost it.
Shaken by echoes that blast the rocks open at dawn,
their hearts crack.
In blue skies vivid as God's grandeur
the pigeons whirl once around
as if to pass on a blessing
for the dwellers of Songbukdong.

In that sterile chasm
where they might seek a patch of yard
to stoop down and peck at a seed,
now driven by the echoing quarry explosions
they leap to the rooftops, at the chimneys
testing the smoky fragrance of morning cooking fires,
then back to the quarry-site, Number 01, the Hill,
to rub their beaks against the warmth
of new-fallen stones.

Pigeons who once saw saintliness
in humankind, a cleaving to humankind
loved, with humans rejoiced in peace;
birds of love and of peace
who now have lost both humans and your hill;
driven out, you cannot stand
even as metaphor
for love or peace.

Having Died

The general becomes a sword
The sovereign becomes a mausoleum
The rich become a fence
The poor become stones and sand.

I would become a cloud,
in the arms of a favoring wind
travel a thousand miles,
rain on the grasses burning
on a tomb.

Summer Mornings After Rain

On days after rain
when the clear sky descends into the pond
and makes a summer morning,
green shadows become paper
and goldfish write poems.

Evening

From so many, one
star looks down at me.
From this many, one
person looks at that star.

As night descends
the star disappears into light
and I disappear into darkness.

Drawn this close
one and one, you and I
become something
that we may meet again.

translated by David R. McCann

NGUYEN CHI THIEN *Socialist Republic of Vietnam*

Planting Peanuts

Peanut seeds were sown, mixed with ash and dung.
To keep prisoners from tasting them
DDT was added.
And did the prisoners touch them?
In the end, tons of peanut seeds were secretly eaten.
Though peanut seeds in the ground
could not sprout
thanks to the 'fertilizer'
the Party announced
that its Winter-Spring project
was successfully completed all the same.

I Kept Silent

I kept silent when I was tortured by my enemy:
With iron and with steel, soul faint in agony —
The heroic stories are for children to believe.
I kept silent because I kept telling myself:
Has anyone, who entered the jungle and who was
    run over by the wild beast
Been stupid enough to open his mouth and ask for mercy?

The Power of Poetry

To me life by day is artificial.
Labouring in shame, usually faint with hunger,
In trivial chatter, I tease away everything.
My release seems unnecessary,
It's only with the coming of the night that I fully
Live, bitterly, past, present and future.
My heart, my brain, tense and intensified
Bearing the blossoming buds and poetry.
My poems, though they may have the shape of flowers,
Explode with a power that is ten thousandfold.

translated by Nguyen Huu Hieu

BUI HOANG CAM   *Socialist Republic of Vietnam*

Six-Years-Old

I

Six-years-old and all alone
He looks for something to eat.
His father, the village landlord,
Had paid his blood-debt to the peasants,
Abandoning him his mother had gone South.

His mother bore him,
He ate, slept on soft bedding,
Wore soft pretty clothes.
He never knew how happy he was.

Then came the storm;
Who could spare thought for such a tiny pawn?
Yet humans will always care for humans;
There will always be compassion.

A wretched, hungry old man
Trembles and shuffles as he hunts for crabs;
He feels pity for this skinny child
Who has neither mother nor father;
He gives him a handful of rice.

Limbs like sticks,
Swollen stomach but scrawny neck, the orphaned child
Surveys the world through round bloodshot eyes:
"I bow to you madam, I beg a bowl of gruel;
please madam, some rice . . ."

Spirits of the Age

II

A young cadre working outside the village
Looks down the road,
Hears his forlorn cry.

She trembles as she recalls
The hunger years of long ago;
Just five-years-old and she must lick
Leaves found in the market-place.

She runs down the lane,
Takes him by the hand and into her house.
From yesterday's supper
She gives him a bowl of rice.

Another girl, of peasant stock
Aspiring to Party membership,
Turns her back to hide her tears:
"A landlord's child, too young to know his fault;
I gave him a bowl of gruel
And they questioned me for three long days."

The land reform cadre recoiled
And gazed at the child, searching for a trace
Of the enemy.
She saw only a child.
The child ate its fill,
Lay down on the ground to sleep.
She thought of the husband she would have
And of their pink, milk-fat children.

III

She lost her job because of it.
In a dark cold room by the light of a lamp
She wrote her confession.

The tongue has no strength
The road is crooked;
The eye is too small
There is no horizon;
The mind is lazy
The color of rusty iron.

Sleeping for years
On the page of a book;
The people are machines
Muscles but no heart.

IV

"In relationship with reactionaries,"
"Loss of revolutionary vigilance."
Night after night she weeps beside the lamp
And asks herself:
"How could I pity the enemy's child?
How happy I would be if I could have
Hated the child!"

translated by David McAree

AHMAD FARAZ *Islamic Republic of Pakistan*

The Mercenaries

Thus far I wrote in praise of you
And now I am ashamed of my songs
I am ashamed for the grace of my verses
I repent the misuse of my poetry
I am ashamed to see my shackled friends
I cannot face my dear ones.

Whenever on my beloved soil swooped
An enemy or the shadow of oppression
Whenever murderers came to attack,
Whenever aggressors crossed the borders
I gave whatever I had,
My blood or my poetic skill

With tearful eyes we bade farewell
When a clarion was blown for you to fight
You sold our honour and saved your life
Victorious you could never be,
But still we never shunned you

The oppressed of the East were ours too,
Whose blood you wiped on your face.
Did you really go to crush revolt
or did you go to plunder and rape?
How could you change their fate?
You were too concerned to change their state!

Whatever the outcome, so be it
the spell of the nightmare is there no more
With arrogance you landed there
With humiliation you laid down your arms:
You went with the ferocity of charging troops,
With yokes and fetters you were taken away.

Still I said you were not to blame
just to cheer up the broken folks
Though my poems were no balm for their wounds
Still I sang for our orphan land,
to comfort my down-trodden people
To console the bleeding hearts

You may recall the day you came
From the enemy's concentration camps
Broken-hearted we lined the streets,
tears in our eyes,
forgetting the bitterness of our humiliation
We showered you with flowers of pride

Little did we know that you the vanquished
Would come to lick our open wounds,
that you who knew the taste of blood
would break all bounds of cruelty,
that after genocide in Bengal
You'd come and slaughter in Bolan.

Why have you put up gallows, oh Ghazis!
across the land
From Qisa Khwani to Manora Island
Why and for whom this butchery,
before whom are you humble, heroes!
which tyrant has ordered you to this,
for whom, heroes!   do you massacre people?

Little did I know, oh sons of bats
You would become a symbol of the dreadful night
Yesterday you waved the flag of the usurper
and today you crawl in the tyrant's court.
For one dictator's sake you hold the sword
against so many necks.

Like the Gurkhas under the British,
brutal and bestial,
like the white mercenaries in Vietnam
who also denounced the freedom-fighters —
You are no different; they too had
rifles, uniforms, names.

You have seen the processions of anguished people,
banners of revolt in their hands.
The drying blood on the pavements
signifies that judgement day is near.
Yesterday we had love for you
but today the flames of hate are rising in our hearts.

Today even the poet must perform his duty.
My pen carries blood, not ink.
Now when you are un-masked, now we know
the hired killers were disguised in soldiers' uniform
No longer just the tyrant's head we want.
we demand the blood of all collaborators!

translated by M.H. Qureshi

FRANK CHIPASULA *Republic of Malawi*

A Lament for Malawi

for Innocent Banda

Give me a kiss, Malawi, my love:
In my mind I shall carry your image
In my heart I shall carry
The deep wound of your love.

Five million caged people languish
in a solid iron fist, speared by a harpoon
Poets tucked away in a police whistle;
The country, folded and stuffed down
A gold magnate's baggy trouser pocket, bleeds
from old rape wounds: In a machila, the tentacled
magnate with his harpoon phallus
aimed between our land's chaste thighs.
Balanced on broken shoulders, lazing in rare
tropical comfort, he puffs like a locomotive head
on a massive corn cob smouldering between
his paper-thin lips. His soul a brittle dollar bill
with the portrait of a slaver and a false gold-
toothed smile sinks roots in our soil.
A cudgel for a walking cane and slave chains
for cuff links, our sweat and blood his jewels
African hide coats his cousin's Holy Bible
bearing the three fiery C's on the great trek
Now their puppet in our skin places his foot
on our mouths and cloggs them with a terrible silence;

He collects millions of eggs for his breakfast table
and throws the shells to us as hunger wrings our bellies.
We fold our arms and die like chickens in a rainstorm;
the brutal saints serve us the bitter wine
from the old goat-skin bags: we take the poison
and we flare against the toy tyrant on the dream throne.
In the caged kingdom we wail in the fist and the whistle.

The Path of the Heart

I

I want to touch again
the warm swollen pulse of song

the drummers' hard palms beat
out of the ancient cowhide drums.

I want to dance the no-space
with swollen bosomed whores

to the loud thuds of drums
grinding to throbbing Simanje manje

wires plucking the heart, setting
the dusty feet on fire with dance

and making blood pound through
our bodies like the Nkula waterfalls

generating a small fire
around which all the people will sit

warming themselves and softly
touching each other on their hearts.

We shall tell stories again
in the womb of a tropical evening.

singing again in unforced harmony
and drinking from the same gourd.

And I long to drink from shebeen
to shebeen in Makhetha, Ndirande.

passing Chibuku beer packets
from mouth to mouth freely

not caring if there are rotting teeth
without fear of Special Branch raids.

II

My country, if this separation is forever
then for heaven's sake, say so; already

my body forgets the warm caress
of your sun, though your rivers

still leap through me
like the flames of your lake

infiltrating your sacred light
into the thickets of my heart

and the sparks prolong my life
and I surrender myself to your fire.

III

My nostrils ache for the sizzling
smell of fish fried over a dried grass fire;

my nostrils itch for fish smoke
as the fire curls the skin off the flesh

and the dripping oils burst into flames
raising the offering to our ancestors.

IV

My feet hanker after the clinging caress
of fresh water swirling around them

like the silken shadow of an aged tree
where I will repose after all this wandering.

I know my heart will always take this path
Back to the land that waits like a lover.

INGOAPELE MADINGOANE *Republic of South Africa*

Black Trial/One

black child
nature's blunder
here i am
lost again
dumped here by the creatures of hell
and left to rot
though worms don't even want me
for they have grown proud
and don't want to hear a thing
about my rotten state

had i known the fruits of being
black as i am
i would have chosen to be
human
so as to avoid the chains of this
black trial

though man has inflicted his grievances
on me
and turned them into this bitterness
that i so resent keep me from hate
for if i hate
i will fall into the valley of hopelessness
and drown like
man

Black Trial/Seven

i have crossed rivers and trudged the
barren plains from the hangman's noose i
have stumbled tripped and fallen hard on
my back hauled myself up and tried once
again to face the world i've never been
knocked out but my soul is still scarred
from the pains sustained and my fingers
still bleed from the cuts received while
trying to get a good grip of my evasive
roots my roots and mine alone

i heard them sing
i heard them sing
oh yes i did

on my homeward way
africa bound
towards sunrise
it was hard
the road was steep
it was heavy
but i heard the beat
and i heard them sing
i heard it blown
the golden horn
i heard the echo
stirring my soul
i heard them cry
tears wetting dry earth
from eyes that have seen
the bitterness of life

i heard those voices
yes i heard them sing
i felt the pain
when my eyes beheld
how man can turn
his fellow men
into beasts of burden
i saw them struggle
i saw them kicked
and saw them die
i heard voices mourn
i heard them sing
when we buried them
i saw them pray
and by god they did
and the tears kept on raining
as they kept on screaming
to man the inflictor to show them mercy
i hit my chest
and a cry escaped my lips
god let it come to an end
i heard them sing
as we filled their graves
with red dusty soil
i heard them sing
as we turned our backs
and walked away

in my lonely room
in the dead of night
the world in repose
i lay still without sleep
and heard those voices
from beyond the grave
i heard them cry
my eyes were wet
i heard them sing
my soul in anguish
i heard them sing
yes i did

Black Trial/Twelve

i talk about me
i am africa
i am the blazing desert yonder
a tall proud grain amidst the sand
egypt my head   the nile my oasis
flow on nile flow on my life-blood
i talk about me
i am africa
i am a man
ogun's image
made from the soil
abibiman
thus
i talk about me
for i am africa

hide and seek i lived
on savanna grasslands
talking freedom
eating salvation
sleeping courage
and
dreaming liberation
for the african soil
thus
i talk about man
i talk about me
for
i am africa

jambo is said as i greeted my father
habari mzuri sana[1] as he nodded in agreement
a sign of love and admiration
wewe unatoka wapi[2] he asked me
this question the ageing poor man
not aware he was talking to his long lost son
mimi ninatoka nchini kwa africa kusini[3]
kula kwa azania[4]
kwa nini wewe umefika hapa[5]
i said *babu nimekuja kuwona ninyi*[6]
in africa the land of your sons
are you in africa is that you *mwana*
he asked
yes *babu* it is me your son
unasema nini he asked me again[7]
hapana maneno i answered[8]
he said
hail *ogun*
hail *abibiman*
land of my sons
sons of my soil
bed of my roots
roots of man
man son of africa
i want you
back
back home in africa
when i lost you
you were a virgin rich with love
until they split your loins
eagle spread and raped you all

within three centuries
when they boasted their manhood and
you abandoned their first child
in the remote trans
kei
oh child land of my sons
come back home to africa
come back home azania my child
give up your prodigal life
don't go flirting again
maybe in *bophutamokete*
this time
come child
land of my sons
sons of the soil
bed of my roots
roots of man
man son of africa

[1] *what news? Very good*
[2] *where do you come from?*
[3] *i come from the land of africa in the south*
[4] *that (land of) azania*
[5] *why have you come here?*
[6] *father, I have come to see you*
[7] *what do you say?*
[8] *without words*

Spirits of the Age

Black Trial/Nineteen

say how beautiful
run the rows
of your plaited hair
mosadi hee mosadi

mosadi say how smart
is *sefaga seo* around your neck
how womanly is the fold
of your dock mosadi

mosadi hee mosadi say what a counsellor
is that african emblem
on your dress mosadi

mosadi say mosadi how bright your face looks
with those wooden earrings
and how warm your breast is
or that man in africa who so much
loves you mosadi

mosadi hee mosadi what is it that you want
when love man   beauty
and home as well as your roots
are in the soil
you are now standing on
mosadi

BIOGRAPHICAL NOTES

These notes were compiled from information provided by the *Index on Censorship*, *Smoloskyp*, and *The Greenfield Review*.

MONA ELAINE ADILMAN   *Editor*

Mona Elaine Adilman is a contemporary Canadian poet who lives in Montreal. A writer of international sensibility, her free-lance articles on environmental and political issues have been widely published. She has taught Ecology and Literature at Concordia University. Recent work is included in *Women on War* (Simon & Schuster, 1988). *Piece Work* and *Nighty-Knight* are among her many books of poems.

CLARIBEL ALEGRIA   *Republic of El Salvador*

Claribel Alegría, one of Central America's best-known poets, was born in Esteli, Nicaragua in 1924, but she considers herself Salvadorean because she went to live in El Salvador when she was a year old. She went to the United States in 1943 and earned her BA from George Washington University. While not originally a political exile from El Salvador, her opposition to successive regimes there has meant she cannot safely return. She now lives in Mallorca. Her books of poetry include a selected poems, *Suma Y Sigue*, her translations of North American poets, *Neuvas Voces de Norte-America*, and *Flowers from the Volcano*.

In 1978, Claribel Alegría was awarded the Casa de las Américas Prize in Havana, Cuba.

SAMIH AL-QASIM   *Arab Republic of Egypt*

Al-Qasim, a Druse Arab born in Jordan in 1939, is committed to the idea of a secular democratic state. He has been confined to prison a number of times after giving poetry readings, and has been placed under house arrest for long periods of time. He continues to live in Haifa where he writes for al-Itthad and al-Jadid.

Some of his numerous collections of poetry include: *Stations of the Sun* (1958), and *Waiting for the Thunderbird* (1969). He also published a verse play, *Quirquash (1970), and On the Political Position and Art: My Life, Cause and Poetry (1970).*

JORGE VALLS ARANGO   *Republic of Cuba*

Jorge Valls Arango was born in Havana, Cuba, 2 February 1933. In 1952, when Batista carried out his coup d'état, Valls spoke out against the dictator and led the struggle from the University. Persecuted and imprisoned, he later went into exile. Upon his return to Cuba in January 1959, he denounced the new form of dictatorship which had come to power under Fidel Castro. Valls Arango was arrested by the political police on 8 May 1964, and sentenced to twenty years of imprisonment.

While in prison, Valls became one of the group of prisoners known as *plantados* — those who refused to accept political indoctrination in return for better treatment. During the worst moments of prison, Valls felt on the verge of complete psychological collapse. The fact that he did not go mad, he attributed to "the hand of God," but also to the writing of poetry and philosophy. "Intellectual production was a means of affirming my humanity," Valls Arango has remarked." "Of every hundred lines we wrote, only one got out of prison." What did survive was smuggled out in what prisoners called 'the way of the rats.' We would drop a piece of paper somewhere, someone else would pick it up, take it further on, then drop it again — until it was finally passed to someone outside the prison."

Jorge Valls was released 18 June 1984, and now lives in New York. He visited Europe to receive the Rotterdam Poetry Festival Prize which had been awarded to him in 1983.

MEEM ATASH   *Islamic Republic of Iran*

Meem Atash, a poet and a former school teacher, was purged in 1980. He is now in hiding in Iran. His books of poems include *Sweet Calls* and *Strange Cities.*

BUI HOANG CAM   *Socialist Republic of Vietnam*

Born in 1922 in Hai-duong province, northern Vietnam, Bui Hoang Cam was an officer in the Vietnamese People's Army during the war against the French colonial power. He was best known among the nationalists and the communists for his patriotic poems. However, after North Vietnam's independence in 1954, he became increasingly critical of the Communist government and the Party, because of the lack of freedom, the corruption and the excesses during the land reform campaign of 1954-6 when thousands of land-owning families and members of the middle classes were either imprisoned or executed.

Following a brief period of artistic freedom called the 'Hundred Flowers Movement' in 1956-8, the government cracked down on writers, artists, and other intellectuals. Many were arrested and sentenced to long-term imprisonment, others were sent to so-called re-education camps.

Bui Hoang Cam was forbidden to write. He and his family have suffered continual harassment from the authorities during the past 25 years. On 20 August 1982, Cam was arrested in Hanoi for having given a manuscript of his new poems to a Vietnamese visitor from Canada. Reported to be suffering from chronic asthma and a serious heart disease, his present whereabouts are unknown.

FRANK CHIPASULA *Republic of Malawi*

Frank Chipasula exemplifies young Malawian writers for whom exile seems the only option. He first experienced censorship while studying literature at Chancellor College, University of Malawi.

For several years, Chipasula worked as a freelance broadcaster for the Malawi Broadcasting Corporation. There, he helped to initiate and sustain "Literature Magazine," a program of original Malawian creative writing. "The Censorship Board is well-known among Malawian writers," Chipasula has remarked. "We therefore exercised self-censorship which was terribly damaging to creative work."

Frank Chipasula is currently a Ph.D. student in English literature and Teaching Fellow in the Afro-American Studies Program, Brown University, United States of America. He has edited two anthologies of poetry: *A Decade in Poetry* (Zambian poetry), and *When My Brothers Come Home* (Central and South African poetry).

ROQUE DALTON *Republic of El Salvador*

Roque Dalton was born in El Salvador in 1933. He studied law and anthropology, was persecuted and imprisoned in his own country, and subsequently lived in exile in Guatemala, Mexico, Czechoslovakia and Cuba. He was murdered in 1975 after returning to help organize the guerrilla struggle.

In October 1981 his two sons disappeared after abduction, victims of the Salvadorean armed forces and related para-military groups.

His book *Taberna Y Ot Ros Lugares* won the Casa de las Américas Prize in Cuba in 1969.

MAHMUD DARWISH   *State of Israel (Palestine)*

Mahmud Darwish was born in 1941 in al-Binwih, a village that was to become part of the new Jewish state in 1949. From a very early age he gave expression to the aspirations of the Arabs. He was put in jail under house arrest, and in 1971 left for the Soviet Union.

Darwish is presently a member of the Palestine National Council and lives in Beirut, where he edits Shu'un Filastinyah, an Arabic monthly dealing with Palestinian affairs.

Some of this poetical works include *Birds Without Wings* (1960), *Olive Leaves* (1964), *Lover From Palestine* (1966) and *The Music of Human Flesh* (1980).

AHMAD FARAZ   *Islamic Republic of Pakistan*

Ahmad Faraz, born in 1936 in Kohat, North-West Frontier Province, is perhaps one of the greatest living poets writing in Urdu. Faraz uses the age-old Ghazal form, which provides the poet with a lavish store of ready-made images, symbols, and metaphors. This brought him almost immediate acclaim, particularly among the young, who felt in his writings the echo of their own heartbeat.

In 1977, when General Zia ul-Hag declared Martial Law, Ahmad Faraz was Director-General of the Academy of Letters. Following the army shooting of students, he wrote a now famous poem (*The Mercenaries*) in protest. He was immediately arrested and put in solitary confinement for over a month without charge or trial. Four months later he was dismissed from his post at the Academy.

ALAIDE FOPPA   *Republic of Guatemala*

Alaide Foppa, university lecturer, art critic, translator, poet, feminist and broadcaster, disappeared in Guatemala City on 19 December 1980. Although the Guatemalan government claimed it was guerrillas who had captured her for ransom money, eyewitnesses state that it was an army commando unit which forced her from her mother's car. Her husband almost fell victim to a similar abduction attempt in 1978, and her journalist son was forced to leave Guatemala in 1980 after his name figured on right-wing death squad lists.

Foppa was a humanist voice in a region of violence. Aged 64 at the time of her abduction, she had been living in exile in Mexico City since the overthrow of President Arbeuz's reformist government in 1954. Until her disappearance Alaide Foppa lectured in literature at the University of Mexico and wrote art criticism for the newspapers. She was also a distinguished translator of Italian, French and English literature. A leading member of Amnesty International, she worked to support women's rights, helping to found *FEM*, Mexico's first feminist magazine. She was also an active supporter of the indigenous women of Guatemala in their struggle against the ethnocidal policies of successive governments.

Las Palabres Y El Tiempo (Words and Time) is the collection of her poems published shortly before her disappearance.

JUAN GELMAN   *Argentine Republic*

Juan Gelman was born in 1930 in Buenos Aires, Argentina. He left his university studies in chemistry "to become a poet," and has since travelled widely. He worked at odd jobs until becoming a journalist. As a member of the Argentine left, which he joined in 1946, he was imprisoned in 1963. Gelman has published seven books of poems, including *Violin Y Ot Ras Cuestiones* (1956), *Fabulas* (1971) and *Colara Buey* (1971).

JUAN FRANCISCO GUTIERREZ   *Republic of Nicaragua*

Juan Francisco Gutiérrez has suffered imprisonment and exile due to his active involvement with political groups opposed to the Somoza dictatorship. Because he has published so little of his work and lives with his family in San José, Costa Rica, Gutiérrez's poetry has, for the most part, been overlooked by his compatriots.

JAVIER HERAUD   *Republic of Peru*

Javier Heraud was born in Lima, Peru, in 1942. He studied at the Universidad Catolica and wrote two books of poems, *El Réo* and *El Viaje*, published posthumously. He joined the guerrilla movement in Peru and died in 1962 at the shore of the river Madre de Dios, fighting against the police.

LOTHAR HERBST *Polish People's Republic*

Lothar Herbst is a poet, essayist, and lecturer at the University of Wroclaw. He was president of the local section of the Union of Polish writers from 1980 until the Union was banned in 1983. Before August 1980 he took part in the activities of the 'Flying University,' the unofficial educational movement. As an independent publisher he has printed over twenty books in a series called *Bibliotek Agony*.

After the imposition of martial law in December 1981, Lothar Herbst was interned in three different camps. In Opolska he was badly beaten. Since his release he has been subjected to constant pressure and harassment by the Polish secret police.

His poem "Letter 7" has appeared in the anthology *Witness Out of Silence: Polish Poets Fighting for Freedom* (Poets' and Painters' Press, London 1980). Its beginning — "I am swallowed up by darkness . . ." acquired a new meaning recently: Lothar Herbst is in a prison hospital, in danger of going blind.

VLADIMIR HOLAN *Czechoslovak Socialist Republic*

Vladimír Holan was born in 1905 and is respected as one of the greatest poets of his generation. Like his friend Seifert, he has been prohibited from publishing his work by the government authorities, and some of his *oeuvre* remains unpublished to this day.

RASHID HUSAYN *State of Israel (Palestine)*

Rashid Husayn was a leading member of the first generation of Arabs to assert their identity and voice their protest inside the Jewish state. He was editor-in-chief of *al Fajr*, an Arabic monthly published by the "Left Zionist" Mapam Party. Occasionally he also contributed in Hebrew to *Ha 'Olam Hazeh*. His poetry readings were heard by Palestinian and Hebrew alike.

Husayn was arrested and jailed several times by the Israeli authorities, and in the mid 1960s he moved to the United States of America. He was found dead of smoke inhalation caused by his own cigarettes on 1 February 1977 after a fire had broken out in his apartment. At the time he was the UN correspondent for WAFA, the Palestinian New agency.

His volumes of poetry include *With the Dawn* (1957), *Rockets* (1958) and *I Am The Land: Do Not Deny Me Rain* (1975).

MANG KE *People's Republic of China*

Mang Ke, born in 1950, was a Young Pioneer (the Chinese Communist Party youth organisation) when he was fifteen. He started to write poetry when he was twenty. During the Peking Spring of 1978-79 when there was some liberalisation in the arts and literature, he founded *Jinitian (Today)*, a literary magazine.

By mid 1979, most of the leaders of the Peking Spring had been arrested and sentenced to long terms of imprisonment for so-called counter-revolutionary activities. *Jinitian* was banned at the end of 1980, and members of the group dispersed and went underground.

IVA KOTRLA *Czechoslovak Socialist Republic*

Iva Kotrlá, poet and mother of five children, was harassed and called to interrogation by the government for the offence of writing poetry, only a few weeks after the birth of her fifth baby. While still in hospital, her home was searched and all her writing since 1966 confiscated.

KIM KWANGSOP *Democratic People's Republic of Korea*

Kim Kwangsŏp, born in 1905 in the northeastern part of what is now North Korea, attended Waseda University in Tokyo, and graduated from the English department. After returning to Seoul and teaching at a high school there for several years, he was arrested in 1941 and imprisoned for three years by the Japanese authorities. (Korea was administered by the Japanese from 1910 to 1945). A leading member of the Korean literary world in the 1950s and 1960s, Kwangsŏp received many prizes, including the Korean Academy of Arts Prize in 1974.

In 1965, Kim suffered a cerebral hemorrhage. In the forward to his 1969 volume of poems, *The Pigeons of Songbukdong*, he wrote that the poems in the collection were written as a result of that illness. He acknowledged that the collection might be his last, but went on to say that "Though I cannot actually return to the spirit in which I wrote these poems, trying to fathom the state in which I found myself after lying in coma for a week . . . . I rejoice at being able to meet again all those friends whose devotion at that time helped to sustain me."

That sense of joy in life and acceptance of death is found in many of the poems in the book. It is a collection that is both profoundly serene and disquieting. Kim Kwangsŏp died in 1977.

ABDELLATIF LAABI *Kingdom of Morocco*

Abdellatif Laâbi, leading Morrocan poet writing in French today, founder of journals, political militant, and translator of Palestinian writers, is perhaps better known outside North Africa as one of Morocco's most prominent political prisoners. His most recent book, *The Poem Beneath the Gag*, looks back to his prison experiences and to the political beliefs that led to his arrest in March 1972, when he was condemned to ten years in prison for "breach of internal security."

Abdellatif Laâbi was not imprisoned for any specific activity or political act. He had been a member of a small but significant intellectual current amongst the Moroccan intelligentsia, which King Hassan's regime considered to be subversive.

According to Laâbi, among the prisoners, "those who wrote poems were the most troubled. They struggled against the door, the walls, the law of silence."

Eventually, in July 1980, he was amnestied. His poetry remains banned in Morocco.

INGOAPELE MADINGOANE *Republic of South Africa*

Ingoapele Madingoane is one of South Africa's leading young black poets, widely known for the dramatic performances of his poetry from memory. Born in Sophiatown in 1950, Madingoane now lives and works in Soweto; he is known in the South African press as "the poet laureate of Soweto."

Although best known as an oral poet, publication of Madingoane's first collection, *Africa My Beginning* (Ravan Press, Johannesburg, 1979, and Rex Collings, London, 1980), proved the effectiveness of his poetry on the printed page. The collection also introduced Madingoane to a wider audience. After an instant sale of 2,000 copies, the book was banned in South Africa.

Madingoane is cautious about committing his poems to paper, for the authorities have on several occasions confiscated his manuscripts.

RAAD MUSHATAT *Republic of Iraq*

Raad Mushatat is one of the countless Iraqi poets and intellectuals who have fled imprisonment, torture and death in their country. His identity is masked by a pseudonym. Even the publishers of his poetry omit their name on the book for fear of reprisals. For the past six years in exile, Raad

Mushatat has been on the move, searching for a country where he can feel safe and where he can write.

AHMED FOUAD NEGM   *Arab Republic of Egypt*

Ahmed Fouad Negm was born in 1929 in the Egyptian countryside. The death of his father when he was six forced him into a life of hardship that was to see him work as a domestic servant, laundry boy, footballer, hawker, tailor, and construction worker.

From 1951 to 1956, while working as a labourer on the railways, Negm rediscovered the Egyptian countryside. The scenes of endemic poverty, deprivation, unemployment, and suffering were to become the subject of many of his lyrics. The songs of the *fellaheen*, their proverbs and sayings, and their characteristic way of describing their life in almost paradoxical epigrams, left a lasting imprint on his style.

In 1959, his trade union activities led to his arrest. While in prison, his first collection of lyrics entitled *Scenes from Life and Prison* was smuggled out and published, earning him a literary prize and limited recognition.

Soon after his release, Negm met the old blind singer, Sheikh Imam. Imam proceeded to put Negm's lyrics to music, synthesising two great traditions: Qur'an recital and peasant group songs. Negm proceeded to write more melodic lyrics.

A widening circle of friends began to promote their songs. The students of the Cairo universities started asking them to appear and sing on the campuses, and the cassette tapes of their songs began finding their way to student gatherings and left-wing circles in the Arab world.

Ahmed Fouad Negm is the only Arab lyricist whose works could reach the four corners of the Arab world despite a wall of silence diligently constructed by the official media. His lyrics are a social comment on the corruption of official life. Negm's constant refusal to bow either to the pressure or to the inducements of the Egyptian authorities made him for almost two decades a frequent victim of harassment, prolonged detention, and torture. He is now in prison after being convicted for 'invading' the Ain-Shams University campus in Cairo and 'assaulting' the police.

IRINA RATUSHINSKAYA   *Union of Soviet Socialist Republics*

Irina Ratushinskaya was arrested in 1982, and convicted in March 1983 of "anti-Soviet agitation and propaganda" — for writing articles and documents of an "anti-Soviet" nature, and through the "manufacture and dissemination'' of her poetry. While in prison she was repeatedly put in solitary confinement for protesting against camp conditions and the treatment of her fellow inmates. Irina Ratushinskaya was released in October 1986, after serving four years of a twelve-year sentence.

Her poetry has been published in English translations in *Poems* (Hermitage, 1984), and her prison memoirs have been collected under the title *Grey is the Color of Hope* (Quality Paperback, 1989).

MAURICIO REDOLES *Republic of Chile*

Mauricio Redolés was born in Santiago, Chile, and studied law in Valparaíso. After the 1973 coup he spent twenty months in prison, and was expelled from Chile in 1975. He went to England, where he studied Sociology.

His poems have been published in magazines and anthologies in Latin America and Europe. He has been heard in song and poetry performance in England, Scotland, Holland, France, and Belgium.

MAURICIO ROSENCOF *Oriental Republic of Uruguay*

Mauricio Rosencof, one of the leading dramatists of Uruguay's independent theatre movement of the 1960s, was arrested in May 1972 and accused of being a member of the Tupamaros guerilla group (a charge on which he has never been tried). A journalist and actor, he had begun to write plays in the late 1950s, all of them rooted in the day-to-day life of Uruguay's ordinary people — workers, shanty-town dwellers, and rural labourers.

After his arrest Rosencof was so savagely tortured that over a period of several months he was taken three times to the Montevideo Military Hospital in a coma. While imprisoned he received very little medical attention — losing control of his reflexes and suffering from deteriorating mental health.

Rosencof was released in April of 1985, having served 13 years in prison.

MYKOLA RUDENKO *Union of Soviet Socialist Republics*

Mykola Rudenko was born on 19 December 1920 into a miner's family in the industrial region of the Ukraine known as ''Donbas.'' His early years can serve as a model for any patriotic Soviet citizen. When war broke out in 1939 he fought in a cavalry regiment, and became a political officer in blockaded Leningrad. He was severely wounded and spent about a year in hospital.

After demobilization in 1946, Rudenko published his first collection of poetry. He was appointed chief editor of the Kiev literary journal, *DNIPRO*, and elected secretary of the Ukrainian Union of Writers. He published over thirty books, including novels, poetry, drama, a collection of stories and fiction, *White Acacia*(1962), and a science-fiction novel, *The Magic Boomerang*(1966). The last collection of poems to be published in the Soviet Union was *The Universe Within You*(1968).

In the 1970s Rudenko began to challenge Soviet government policies. In a *samizdat* essay, "How to Save the Sun," he exposed social and economic conditions in the Ukraine. Finally, he was not allowed into print, and lost his livelihood. He joined the human rights movement, becoming a member of the Moscow branch of Amnesty International in 1975. One year later, he became head of the Ukrainian Helsinki Monitoring group. He was arrested, expelled from the Communist Party and the Ukrainian Writers' Union, and on 30 June 1977 he was sentenced to seven years imprisonment and five years internal exile.

For a time he was forcibly confined to a Kiev psycho-neurological clinic where he wrote the dramatic poem *The Cross* (1976). This work describes the Great Famine of 1933 and draws a parallel between Ukraine's tragedy and the Crucifixion of Christ.

Rudenko served his imprisonment in labour camps where, in spite of his disability, he was deprived of invalid status. In 1986 he was joined in exile by his wife, Raisa Rudenko, who had been serving a prison term for "anti-Soviet agitation and propaganda." Rudenko declared a hunger-strike in support of the demand that he and his wife be released immediately and permitted to emigrate.

On 20 May 1987, Mykola and Raisa Rudenko were released from internal exile.

JAROSLAV SEIFERT *Czechoslovak Socialist Republic*

Jaroslav Seifert's poetry has been one of the cornerstones of Czech national culture for more than half a century. The censorship imposed on his works indicates that one need not be a militant adversary or outspoken opponent of the regime to be persecuted by the totalitarian state.

Seifert played an important role at the time of the Prague Spring in 1968 when he was elected President of the Czechoslovakia Writers' Union. His poetry was banned for ten years, circulating only in typewritten *Samiszat* editions. In 1984 he was awarded the Nobel Prize for literature.

Three months before his death, Seifert was forced to remove his name from the Charter 77 document which read: "Is there not something monstrous about conditions in a country in which creative freedom can only be enjoyed by those who are prepared to risk imprisonment?"

Most recent collections of his work include *The Plague Column* and *Umbrella From Picadilly*.

AHMAD SHAMLOU   *Islamic Republic of Iran*

Ahmad Shamlou is a well known poet in Iran. He was dismissed from the Ministry of Culture in 1980 and is now in hiding. *The Game is Over* was published shortly before the fall of the Shah.

SAEED SOLTANPOUR   *Islamic Republic of Iran*

Saeed Soltanpour, an Iranian poet and playwright, was executed on 26 July 1981 by the authorities of the Islamic Republic. He was imprisoned many times under the Shah's regime, mostly for his writings. His books of poems included *Books of Ballads From Jail*. A founding member of Iran's Theatre Society in 1968, his plays were often banned. His last play was called *Koshtargah (Slaughter House)*. He was elected to the Executive Committee of the Writers' Association of Iran in 1980.

The poem in this anthology was recited by Soltanpour in front of a huge crowd during a public event called "Ten Nights of Poetry" in November 1977 held at the Goethe Institute and organised by the Writers' Association of Iran.

VASYL STUS   *Union of Soviet Socialist Republics*

Vasyl Stus is one of the leading Ukrainian poets of his generation. He died in a Soviet prison camp in September 1985. Stus was a leading representative of the "sixties," a group of literary intellectuals who spearheaded a revival of Ukrainian cultural and civic life during the 1960s.

Vasyl Stus was arrested on 12 January 1982, during the KGB crackdown against Ukrainian human rights activists. He was imprisoned for "anti-Soviet agitation and propaganda," and for allowing his poetry to be published in the West. Despite intolerable conditions, he continued to write poems and translate prolifically from German (Goethe, Rilke, and Brecht). These were confiscated.

In the fall of 1975 Stus sent a statement from the Mordovian labour camp, accusing the KGB of making his people "tongueless and voiceless."

He declared that the judicial trials of 1972 and 1973 were "trials against human thought, against the process of thinking, itself, against humanism and against manifestations of filial love for one's nation." He renounced his Soviet citizenship at the end of 1978. "To be a Soviet citizen means to be a slave."

When exiled in 1979, Stus joined the Ukrainian Helsinki monitoring group, and was re-arrested on 9 May 1980. In camp he had surgery to remove over half his stomach, but was forced to fulfill his work quota in the mines.

Stus's second term of imprisonment involved ten years in a special regime camp and five years of internal exile. During the trial it was revealed that Stus had been tortured during the investigation. In addition to his earlier illnesses (stomach, heart, injured legs) he began to exhibit dangerous symptoms of a serious kidney malfunction. For an entire year he was held in an isolation cell on reduced rations. In a rare document called "Camp Notes" he wrote: "We have lost all rights to belong to ourselves. I feel like a walking corpse. They say when God wants to punish someone he takes away his mind."

NGUYEN CHI THIEN   *Socialist Republic of Vietnam*

Nguyen Chi Thien is a poet who was first detained in 1959 for speaking against the authorities. He is reported to have spent the past twenty years of his life in various prison camps. In 1979 a collection of his poems was smuggled out of North Vietnam. In a covering letter, he implored the world outside to publicize the conditions in the prison camps. Nguyen Chi Thien's present fate or whereabouts are unknown.

ARMANDO VALLADARES   *Republic of Cuba*

Armando Valladares Pérez was imprisoned in Cuba for 21 years before his release in 1982. Valladares was tried for "offences against the powers of the state," including possession of gelignite and firearms.

Some years after his imprisonment, Armando Valladares began to write poetry, which he smuggled out of jail to his wife Martha in Miami, Florida. It was published in 1976 in Miami as *Desde Mi Silla de Ruedas (From My Wheelchair)*, and included in a book on his case, *Prissonnier de Castro (Prisoner of Castro)*, published in France in 1979.

Valladares remained in prison largely because of this writing and its publication abroad. The fact that he was a *plantado*, one of about 250 prisoners who refused to accept the authorities' rehabilitation program of obedience to prison regulations and work, is doubtless also a factor. In 1974 Valladares was one of a group of prisoners in La Cabana prison in Havana who refused to wear the uniforms of common criminals. During this protest he contracted polyneuritis as the result of vitamin deficiency and lost the use of his legs.

In April 1980 Armando Valladares was taken to the Combinado des Este prison near Havana, where he has spent time both in solitary confinement and the prison hospital. As well as polyneuritis he is suffering from polmonary emphysema and asthma. He is denied visits from his family or correspondence.

JAN VLADISLAV   *Czechoslovak Socialist Republic*

Jan Vladislav, a distinguished poet, essayist and translator, since 1948 has been prohibited from publishing either poetry or criticism. He has instead devoted himself to the translation of poetry. He began publishing his own series of unofficial typescript editions called *kvart* (quarto). He was forced into exile in 1981, and now lives in Paris.

JAN ZAHRADNICEK   *Czechoslovak Socialist Republic*

Jan Zahradníček, an important Catholic lyricist, was sentenced to thirteen years imprisonment in the 1950s for alleged treason. Released shortly before his death in 1960, Zahradníček was later "rehabilitated." While in prison, he wrote his major work, *Sign of Power* as well as two collections, *Four Years* and *House of Fear*, none of which have been published in Czechoslovakia since 1968.

"The Mercenaries" by Ahmad Faraz. Vol. 14, No. 4, 1985, pp. 34–35.

"Time" and "Words" by Alaide Foppa. Vol. 13, No. 3, 1984, pp. 19–20.

"Exile" by Juan Gelman. Vol. 16, No. 7, 1987, p. 22.

"III," "XVI" and "XXIII" by Mang Ke. Vol. 12, No. 6, 1983, p. 18.

"Under the Skin," "At Moments of Piety," and "Growing Up" by Iva Kotrlà. Vol. 14, No. 5, 1985.

"They Came Looking for You," "Heresy," and "Poems Beneath the Gag (I)" by Abdellatif Laabi. Vol. 11, No. 1, 1982, p. 22.

"Black Trial/seven," "Black Trial/twelve," and "Black Trial/nineteen" by Ingoapele Madingoane. Vol. 13, No. 3, 1984, p. 37.

"Many Dresses" and "Three Iraqi Women, 1979" by Raad Mushatat. Vol. 15, No. 2, 1986, pp. 30–31.

"Prisoner's File" by Ahmed Fouad Negm. Vol. 9, No. 2, 1980.

"Press Conference," "The Future Will Return," and "Otters" by Mauricio Redoles. Vol. 14, No. 4, 1985, pp. 47–48.

"My dockyard sends you this boat, love," "Do you know, little daughter," "They covered the light," and "Fingers" by Mauricio Rosencof. Vol. 11, No. 1, 1982, p. 27.

"It's so easy: just recant" by Mykola Rudenko. Vol. 8, No. 1, 1979 p. 38.

"On this shore of fear" by Saeed Soltanpour. Vol. 11, No. 6, 1982 p. 6.

"The game is over" by Ahmad Shamlou. Vol. 12, No. 3, 1983 p. 28.

"Planting Peanuts," "I Kept Silent," and "The Power of Poetry" by Nguyen Chi Thien. Vol. 11, No. 3, 1982, p. 8.

"Planted in My Chair," "Wings Will Grow One Day," "Christmas," "Situation," and "Over the Wires" by Armando Valladares. Vol. 11, No. 2, 1982, pp. 10–13.